The Prettiest Woman

Forerunners: Ideas First

Short books of thought-in-process scholarship, where intense analysis, questioning, and speculation take the lead

FROM THE UNIVERSITY OF MINNESOTA PRESS

(Continued on page 96)

The Prettiest Woman
Nostalgia for Late Industrial
Capitalism

Grant Farred

University of Minnesota Press

MINNEAPOLIS

LONDON

ISBN 978-1-5179-1832-3 (PB)
ISBN 978-1-4529-7206-0 (Ebook)
ISBN 978-1-4529-7433-0 (Manifold)

Published by the University of Minnesota Press, 2025
111 Third Avenue South, Suite 290
Minneapolis, MN 55401–2520
www.upress.umn.edu

Available as a Manifold edition at manifold.umn.edu

The University of Minnesota is an equal-opportunity educator and employer.

This book is dedicated to my uncles:
In Death, as In Life.

James Roland Farred
26 March 1941 – 21 November 2020
Man of Science, Elemental Being, Gymnast, Angler

W. Arthur Farred
6 May 1943 – 10 June 2010
Gifted Exponent of the Art of the *Voyous,*
West-Facing in His Inclinations

Godfrey Thomas Fisher
11 December 1941 – 5 May 2008
Gentle in Disposition, He Bore Life as He Could

Contents

Like Clockwork: "Bring the Jobs Back to America"

THE PERFIDIOUSNESS OF IT ALL. The political deceit at the core of US nostalgia for late industrial capitalism.

You can count on it. Every two years, in the buildup to elections in the United States, you can be sure of it. It matters not that the cry seems ever more plaintive. Or that it grows, simultaneously, ever more muffled and irrepressible with every election cycle. Or that it appears ever more duplicitous. Or that it reeks of desperation. Or that it is grows ever more anachronistic. It persists. Even if they code their promises differently—and even that it is a claim that ranks as rhetorically dubious—both major US political parties subscribe to the logic of economic return. That is, under this Democratic administration or that Republican one, manufacturing jobs will, through some miracle, return to America. America, a country that "used to make things," will revitalize its manufacturing base.

Neither political party ever details how this manufacturing base will be restored. No matter; it is a promise that must be made. Even as everyone knows it cannot be kept. This economic appeal is addressed to that mythical figure: the middle-class, white, heteronormative blue-collar worker, that salt-of-the-earth figure, all over the country, but is especially aimed at the Midwest. A Midwest that is by no means geographically (geopolitically) limited to the heartland states—of which Ohio, Indiana, Illinois, and Michigan can be said to constitute the core. In truth, however, this fictitious Midwest can begin much further east. Say, from old mill towns in Rhode Island or western Massachusetts, running through now-crumbling small to midsize cities in upstate New York—Utica, Rochester, Buffalo[1]—to Erie, Pennsylvania, and relentlessly on to Pittsburgh, Cleveland, Gary, with the economic rot reaching its low point in Detroit. Somehow it is always Detroit that is held up as the archetype of industrial decay. Detroit, home of the US auto industry, Ford, General Motors, is the face of industrial devastation. Detroit, where automation made the assembly line obsolete. Detroit, bested in the 1970s by a Japanese car industry that was leaner, more efficient (making smaller cars as opposed to US gas guzzlers), and technologically forward looking.

The United States' old industrial base, now perceived, correctly, as ravaged by global capital's relentless march away from manufacturing and in the direction of a technological revolution, is relentless in its pursuit of ever greater efficiency, which has the commensurate effect of requiring increasingly less labor and, it is presumed, a set of skills vastly different from that which allowed US industry to flourish after World War II. The much lamented "boom years" ended somewhere in the early 1970s, if the neoliberal account of postindustrialism's rise is to be believed. The

---

1. Rochester and Buffalo, I should note, have both undertaken urban renewal projects, projects that have, to this point, been more successful in some areas than others. The waterfront in Buffalo, for example, has revitalized parts of the city's downtown. Areas of urban blight remain visible in Rochester.

OPEC oil crisis of 1972 figures prominently in this narrative of US industrial decline.

From the 1970s on, the effects of deindustrialization have provided rhetorical fodder for the campaign trail. Until 2016, this discourse appeared to have peaked some twenty years earlier, with the election of Bill Clinton. A cruel irony, of course, because it was this self-same Clinton who, despite having sung the praises of working stiffs on the campaign trail, oversaw the implementation of the North American Free Trade Agreement (NAFTA—integrating the economies of Canada, Mexico, and the United States) on January 1, 1994, thereby further depleting an already emaciated industrial base as the remaining manufacturing jobs moved south. With an unseemly haste. In the cause of lower labor costs.[2]

"The American Worker" and Grievance

The figure of "The American Worker," betrayed by politicians in the pockets of a big capital committed to a service-industry economic model (among which financial services rank first), has endured, is lamented as that American left behind by technological advances. The superannuation by finance capital of an America that makes things is the very issue dramatized, as a later section of this essay shows, by the 1987 movie *Wall Street*,

---

2. It is a refrain that echoes right into our moment, that it is still possible to "Make things in America." All US politicians, it would seem, are intent on forgetting that both parties signed on to the NAFTA agreement, creating a trade zone that extends the length of the continent and then some, no matter that the free-trade agreement was spearheaded by a Democratic president (Bill Clinton), was opposed by labor unions, but nonetheless won majority support in its passage through Congress.

where it is cast as a benign generational tussle. The American whose right to a decent-paying job is every day being denied by the "forces of globalization" (a catchall phrase if there ever was one), the laborer who is now being promised that, yes, manufacturing jobs will be "brought back."

A manufacturing pipe dream. Of course.

Except it is a pipe dream that has, since 2016, assumed a nightmarish visage.

With the election of Donald Trump in 2016, the fantasy of "bringing jobs back" has hardened into a toxic political substance, with frightening consequences for the American body politic. That mythical "blue-collar guy" is now no longer confined to the Rust Belt. (As we have just pointed out, deindustrialization was a national—indeed, a global—rather than a local, "Midwestern" phenomenon.) That mythical figure has metastasized. This figure, now protean in profile, is no longer only based in class. It includes every aggrieved white person in America, from low-wage workers to elected officials (in various states across the country), from those sworn to uphold the law (police officers chief among them) to emergency workers, from small business owners to members of the professional class.

The white aggrieved presents itself as "anti-elite" even as it takes its cues, entirely without irony, from a nonconsecutive second-term president who wouldn't know a hammer from a power drill and who has a long history of stiffing contractors. Among those venerated self-same working men and women (although in Trump's discourse misogyny rules) are, we presume, some who vote for him in significant numbers.

At its core, as currently constituted, is racial animus. An animus augmented and intensified by xenophobia. This animus is easily mobilized because are "coastal elites" held responsible for a deindustrialization that is now no longer regional but racial. (According to this logic, there are no postindustrial capitalists who are truly Midwestern in disposition. In other words, the Koch brothers [Wichita, Kansas], Warren Buffett [Omaha, Nebraska], and their like are, in truth, East Coasters in economic practice—the commitment to profit—even as they retain, somewhere in their gold-plated bosom, in their hearts the unimpugnable values of the heartland.) It is white men, angry white men: white men aggrieved by demographic shifts that threaten their political dominance; angry white men bitter at the rising educational levels and economic power of women, especially highly educated and visible women (making it all too easy to pillory a figure such as Hillary Clinton), to say nothing of women of color; angry white men now, in short, lashing out at an America no longer centered around their economic profile—that American white man presumed to be non–college educated, more rural than suburban, more nominally Christian (of the hold-the-Bible upside down variety), and Second Amendment–oriented than polyglot, racially diverse, urban America; provincial, not global, in outlook.

In short, post-2016 postindustrial America has assumed the face of a white male grievance even as it cannot be restricted to white men. (I have written about how white male grievance is constitutive of and has persisted throughout US history elsewhere. A history of grievance that begins with the Declaration of Independence and has persisted through the Civil War, the violent undoing of the Reconstruction project, the struggle for Civil Rights, and so on, culminating in the event of January 6, 2021.)[3] These angry white men are its violent core, its rampag-

3. See Grant Farred, *Grievance: Aphorisms, Fragments* (Prickly Paradigm Press, 2024).

ing foot soldiers, its chief political constituency. A constituency capable of a violence that has already reached insurrectionary proportions. At least once—January 6—with more such manifestations, it would seem, in the offing. Imminently.

Pretty Woman

Therefore, while this essay takes as its focus the 1990 movie, *Pretty Woman*, it belongs very much to the zeitgeist of our moment. Through this movie, *The Prettiest Woman: Nostalgia for Late Industrial Capitalism* offers a critique of the ways US popular culture grapples with, glamorously, the nostalgia for a mode of life sustained by industrial capitalism that is on its last legs. Maybe even has one foot in the grave already. And yet it persists, this nostalgia—this nostalgia that seems ever more mobilizable. In this way, as much as *The Prettiest Woman* speaks to an earlier postindustrial conjuncture, what is ideologically at stake in this essay remains pertinent.

The ways in which the1990 movie takes up nostalgia for late industrial capitalism is not, of course, of a complete piece with our contemporary. In fact, we could justifiably claim, in hindsight, that the movie's rendering of nostalgia is anachronistic, and in that way a sharp reminder of how the public debate around—and invocation of—that nostalgia has shifted. To address what subtends the movie's nostalgia, this essay shifts registers in the second half. While a Marxist (and cultural Marxist) critique is the dominant thread in the opening half, the second half is inflected by that brand of Lacanian thought practiced by Slavoj Žižek. It is not so much that the historico-materialist is relegated as it is supplemented—sublated, even; *Aufhebung*—by the psychoanalytic so that the "domestic" elements at work in *Pretty Woman*, the patronymic family drama that operates in a lower frequency, can be thought in its specificity.

6

However, this second line of critique in no way detracts from a salient recognition. More than thirty years after Hollywood gave us *Pretty Woman,* America's political nostalgia for late industrial capitalism remains stronger than ever. And, more virulent than it has ever been. Thought against the history that is our history of the present, *The Prettiest Woman* is a reminder most untimely—in Friedrich Nietzsche's sense—of how, when the terms of a longstanding debate change, they rarely, if ever, do so for the better. (That is, if they can even be said to change at all.)

So conceived, *The Prettiest Woman* offers itself as a first (which is never a first) articulation of American nostalgia for late industrial capitalism. As is the case with all first articulations, it is the erasures that mark—and mar—them. Erasures, however, that must be understood as not constitutive philosophical deficiencies but as the fecund ground that is a historical moment's unthought. In this way, it is both that which *Pretty Woman* addresses—the ways in which nostalgia manifests itself in one moment—and that which lies beyond (but not outside) its historical purview that haunts our thinking of capitalism.

As such, *The Prettiest Woman* is a thinking of the nostalgia for late industrial capitalism that is, in and of itself, by itself, because of itself, at once provocative and constitutively insufficient. It might very well be that the salient feature of this essay is that, in turning its focus to an earlier historical moment, it compels us to attend ever more urgently to our contemporary and, in so doing, to sift through the detritus that is the remains of late industrial capitalism. *The Prettiest Woman,* then, as that thinking of the nostalgia for late industrial capitalism circa 1990 that stands as a first tracing through what remains, almost against expectation, of late industrial capitalism. As much as anything, this essay may very well have the unintended effect of making us nostalgic for an earlier, prettier, mode (and moment) of nostalgia. It is an accounting of what has been lost, because we remain, as it seems we always have been, in the thrall of capitalism.

Who knows where we will be two years from now? What will we be nostalgic for then? What kind of dramas about the conjuncture of family dysfunction and the machinations of capital, late industrial and technologically advanced, will pre-occupy us then?

She's a Pretty Woman

> No social order ever perishes before all the productive forc-
> es and the relations of production for which there is room in
> it have developed; and new, higher relations of production
> never appear before the material conditions of their exis-
> tence have matured in the womb in the old society itself.

—KARL MARX, Preface to *A Critique of Political Economy*

SHE'S A SMALLTOWN GIRL FROM GEORGIA. It's around midnight and her shift is just beginning. She, Vivian Ward (Julia
Roberts), is a prostitute working the strip in one of the sleazier
parts of Hollywood. He, Edward Lewis (Richard Gere) is a pri
vate equity financier (PEF—a corporate raider or venture capitalist) from the tonier environs of Long Island, New York. He's
divorced and has proven himself unable to sustain a meaningful
relationship with the women who have passed through his life
since his divorce. Driving his attorney's car, a late-model Lotus
Esprit, our corporate raider is lost. What is worse, the Lotus
Esprit belonging to Philip Stuckey (Jason Alexander) is, as it
should be, a stick shift, which Edward cannot drive. (Surely no
self-respecting car enthusiast even considers purchasing the
automatic version of the Lotus. God forbid. What's the point of

driving an automatic sports car? Where's the fun in not having a manual transmission?)

Even worse is the fact that Edward's ignorance about the layout of Los Angeles has seen him arrive in said seedier part of the city. This is Vivian's neighborhood, where the prostitutes, their pimps, the junkies, the drug dealers, and their ilk hold sway. He is a long way from Philip's Beverley Hills mansion where he was the guest of honor earlier that afternoon.

A lost man needs directions. Vivian knows the urban geography of Los Angeles. They haggle, briefly, over the price of directions. They settle on a price for directions, a price that includes her accompanying him to his very upscale hotel. She is unable to abide his mechanical incompetence—it is a thing of pain for her to hear him try to change gears. Consequently, she asserts her authority and takes over the driver's seat from Edward. And, boy, can this pretty woman drive a stick.

Therewith the scene is set. Seasoned corporate raider meets the prostitute and in Hollywood that must be a love story. And *Pretty Woman* is exactly that. In the terms of this essay, however, the love story is the narrative (Hollywood, if you will) gloss that provides us entrée to the economic substance. Contained within the substance, of course, is the critique of late industrial capitalism. It is a critique that is sometimes, often, submerged within the movie's dominant narrative. At other times it breaks through the veneer, while in still other moments it presents itself, maybe boldly, for our thinking. But, to begin with, we must acknowledge the effect of the gloss, because what a gloss it is.

The swanky Regent Beverley Hills Wilshire hotel, where Edward occupies the penthouse suite whenever he is town, the splendor of the exclusive stores that line Rodeo Drive, the urbane sophistication of a polo match. What does not accord comfortably with this ostentatious display of wealth is the specter of late industrial capitalism. It's the fly in the ointment, this last (or, very close to last) gasp of industrial capitalism, this late but not yet obsolete mode of generating capital through production, that disturbs this otherwise well-modulated, carefully calibrated, PEF surface, which does nothing to disguise the utter ruthlessness of venture capitalism. If Gary Marshall's 1990 *Pretty Woman* is, in the first instance, rich-boy-meets-poor-(prostitute)-girl romance, then it is, in a register lower but perhaps more sonorous, a singular critique of corporate raider capitalism. Its singularity derives from the ways *Pretty Woman* articulates a profound nostalgia for late industrial American capitalism. Late industrial capitalism's last stand.

As if Marx's analysis could not fully account for the unexpected, stubborn, manifestation of the residual. Much as industrial capitalism has, to all intents and purposes, exhausted itself, much as "new, higher relations of [non-]production have come into being," the unwelcome, bastard child that "matured in the womb of the old society itself" insists upon its right to an untimely arrival. Late industrial capitalism, out of joint with the economic modality of the times, would seem to hold with the Pyrrhic logic of "better late than never." In giving voice to late industrial capitalism's untimely manifestation, *Pretty Woman*, inadvertently or not, suggests that there may yet be at least one more "productive force" within industrial capitalism that has not yet been exhausted.

But, like all last stands, it is only a matter of time before there emerges the perfect alignment that Marx expects between the "social order" and the "higher relations of production"; it is but a matter of time before this symmetry is achieved—or restored. Or that there may come into being the congruence between the "social order" and the "higher relations of *non*-production," to phrase the matter as an economic truth. What Marshall's movie stages is that moment of economic and philosophical disruption within the "social order," annotating more than just the impossibility of a seamless transition between economic modalities. Marshall's movie articulates, true to the spirit of nostalgia, the spectral presence of the past as an interrogation of the modality of the present. An interrogation that shades, unsubtly, into an indictment. The question posed by this logic that is felicitous to *Pretty Woman* nostalgia is not (at least not so much), What is this modality that you are upholding? as it is, How could you uphold this nonproductive modality? The force of this interrogative nostalgia is singular. And it is singular because it is, as will see, a resilient rhetorical beast.

Pretty Woman is a tribute to that resilience, and as a rhetorical cinematic device, this nostalgia is possessed of a Hollywood grandeur peculiarly its own. But we should not be mistaken, this nostalgia for late industrial capitalism is less a product of the Hollywood imagination than it is an ideological phenomenon that finds, as noted in the Introduction, an enduring articulation across the American political spectrum. As such, *Pretty Woman*'s nostalgia speaks the irrepressible yearning for that (American) economic modality that we might conceive of as a productive America.

It is a nostalgia for that America where the US economy can be said to "still make something." A fundamentalist economic ideology: you *are* only if you *make*. It is if as Marx's explication of profit, the difference between use and exchange value, had been rendered a matter of no economic consequence. Not even as Marx says in Volume I of *Capital*, a "mixing up of use-value and exchange value."[1] Productivity not only as the only economic virtue, but as the very *raison d'etre* of the (national) economy itself.

---

1. Karl Marx, *Capital: Volume One, A Critique of Political Economy*, ed. Friedrich Engels; trans. Samuel Moore and Edward Aveling (Dover Publications, 2011), 177.

Late industrial capitalism sets itself against the predatory venture capitalism that has, unceremoniously and without apology, put paid to industrial capitalism. The triumph of the postindustrial American economy is nothing but a matter of obeying the law of profit margins. Selling services generates far greater profits than making products. The ways of capitalism are, as Joseph Schumpeter recognized the better part of a century ago, "essentially evolutionary," and, because of that, capitalism must evolve itself or it will "atrophy."[2]

Making productivity a religion is, of course, an economic modality that is raced, even if it cannot be said to be a nostalgia that is the exclusive preserve of white America for the postwar but pre–Civil Rights 1950s political dispensation. But it does belong to that economic moment when the racial order seemed, if only for a moment, firmly entrenched, when working-class white men (sans a college education) could count on good-paying (unionized) jobs, when the booming postwar economy promised a secure future; an economic future brighter for some than for others, needless to say, but a moment of economic stability that would be upended, rudely, a little more than a decade later. Marking, ironically, that moment when the ideology—the belief in racial equality that was now demanded by a black population that had been enlisted in the war against Nazism—that had "matured in the womb of the old society" would come fully into itself. And, as the black nationalist struggle that emerged both in conjunction with and as a critique of Civil Rights discourse, that ideology would extend and radicalize itself—in the formation and activities of the Black Panthers, to name but the most militant example of that ideology incipient within the "womb of the old society."

2. Joseph Schumpeter, *Capitalism, Socialism, and Democracy* (Wilder Publications, Inc., 1942), 145.

Nostalgia

The winter evening settles down
With smell of steaks in passageways.
Six o'clock.
The burnt-out ends of smoky days

—T. S. ELIOT, "Preludes"

NOSTALGIA, in the Lacanian sense, as the impossible desire to retrieve a lost—a love, as it is sometimes figured—object. The object has been made irretrievable to the subject because the object in question is and can never be the same as the object of the subject's desire. Nevertheless, the relationship—the dialectic—that binds—links—subject to object endures, remains, no matter that the nature of the relationship is at the mercy of forces that the subject cannot control. The relationship endures because the subject has cathected itself onto the object—the subject has invested the object with an emotional significance, often a significance disproportionate to the object's "real" value. The object continues to mean to the subject, the subject retains its meaning to the object, regardless, because of the power of the subject's emotional attachment. The effect of cathexis is such that no matter, as Gilles Deleuze would insist, the difference (as it pertains to the object) that overdetermines repetition, the object cannot be overcome. The object of nostalgia, however, is subject to difference in more than one way: not only is the object made different by repetition but the object can now only (in its difference) be located in a distinct time and place—the object has, as it were, moved, relocated, taken up residence in an *other* time, a time that can only be understood as anachronistic, a time inflected with a set of affective and political investments that, as a rule, do not reflect the facticity of the time. Anachronism as the making-ideal-of-the-time-that-was; an idealization that can only be apprehended in its nostalgia, that is, to phrase the matter euphemistically, an idealized nostalgia that comes to take on the status of truth.

Such nostalgia is the desire to cling, against all economic good sense, to that object that is being lost. This is fiction in which fidelity to late industrial capitalism persists. In fact, this mode of capitalist production that is the object of nostalgia, has, already, long since been lost. Nostalgia summoned up, instrumentalized even, as a bulwark against the machinations—if such an industrialist pun might be permitted—of capitalism's imperious forward march. That mode of being that has been put under erasure by technology and the rapacious appetite of vulture capitalism: capitalism as destructive in its entirety, and, as such, rather too destructive of a particular moment. This nostalgia is the desire to safeguard that mode of capitalist production, that moment conceived here as late industrial capitalism, which has, in the main, been rendered redundant but whose moment is not (yet fully) passed, certainly not in its entirety. The rusty remnants of a certain capitalist spirit, exhausted, beaten, but defiant in its refusal to submit to the relentless advance that is postindustrial capital. This is late industrial capitalism as, in Eliot's sense, "the burnt-out ends of smoky days." Nothing left but cinders and ashes, as Jacques Derrida might have it.

These remains—the almost completely erased traces of their economic kind—stand as the last vestiges of a world that has passed. A world that has effectively passed except for those final remnants that are trying, in vain, it would seem, to set themselves against ruin. This nostalgia made of ruins, this nostalgia for the ruins, this nostalgia against the ruination of the ruins. After all, is the effect of postindustrial capitalism not a collection of "burnt-out" industries, economies of former mill towns laid low, manufacturing industries remembered only because the old factories have become the strongholds of drug addicts, the homeless, and youth seeking respite from all forms of authority? Or, old warehouses remodeled as lofts on the upper floors, with coffee shops, niche restaurants, e-bike shops on the ground floor. In other words, out of the ruins of industrial capitalism is born the playground of urban hipsters. All this destruction wrought by industrial capitalism is now made into grist for the mill— pun intended—of the postindustrial and postmodern creative economy.

The postmodern economy is one that is largely alien to the generation that came into adulthood in an economically prosperous postwar America. That generation of white America that fled the city in search of racially segregated suburbia where they would be spared the influx of blacks and other new immigrants who were trying to make a life for themselves in those self-same cities. That generation of mainstream America who barely tolerated the emergent counterculture (the likes of Kerouac, Ginsberg, James Dean, Jimi Hendrix, Marilyn Monroe, James Baldwin, Sly and the Family Stone, and so on) could certainly not conceive of a "creative laboring class," artists, musicians, painters, poets, who turned abandoned factories into living spaces. Abandoned factories transformed into lofts was not what that generation anticipated, the postwar heirs and beneficiaries of the so-called Greatest Generation. With good reason, because theirs was a generation that could not imagine creativity in this new capitalist mode: This new, alien mode of capitalism, this unprecedented form of culture-making, of virtual production, of making an eco-friendly urban life. Of making profit out of the ruins of the world that postindustrial capitalism had destroyed. Of the coming gentrification that would price black Americans and new immigrants out of what had long been their neighborhoods.

All this, we can say, is an American generation's nostalgia for an immanent capitalism. A visible, tangible, productive capitalism; that is, a capitalist economy where products, the things Americans buy, their cars, their washing machines, their refrigerators and their photocopiers, are made in the continental United States. A nostalgia for that economic mode—which is of course also a moment in capitalism—when American cars (Ford, GM, Chrysler) used to roll off the assembly line in Detroit (before the Japanese "invasion," led by Toyota, overtook the US car industry, whereafter Toyota came to dominate the international car market); when steel was manufactured in Pittsburgh and not imported from China; when American ingenuity led the way globally so that the Xerox company of Rochester, New York, was so dominant as to make of "Xerox" as much a product as a verb ("xeroxing"), so synonymous was the work of photocopying with the company's name. That moment when industrial capitalism, in cities such as Cleveland, Ohio, with its manufacturing plants, and Gary, Indiana, with its billowing, polluting smokestacks, guaranteed jobs for white workers. (Jobs that, at least for a couple of generations, offered the security of lifetime employment; hence the term "company town.")

A Hollywood Genealogy

MOVIES SUCH AS (in chronological order and beginning with *Wall Street*, a film which we have already noted [Michael Douglas, Charlie Sheen, Martin Sheen]), *Pretty Woman* and *Other People's Money* (1991, Danny DeVito) stand as the cultural artifacts that pronounce the death of industrial capitalism. Douglas's Gordon Gecko, we remember, gave full-throated voice to the Reaganite zeitgeist. The phrase that will not die, no matter how odious its resonance: "Greed is good." Late industrial capitalism puts its massively devalued stock in, as George H. W. Bush would have phrased it, a "kindler, gentler" capitalism. Capitalist rapacity, union busting, the undoing of the welfare state, all of it was permissible in Bush's conception of beneficent capitalism; capitalism without its harshest Gekko-esque features, without making its ardor for exploitation quite so plain. No need to shout "Greed is good." The more discreet registers will do as well. Subtlety, understatement: that behavior which befits a Skull and Bones man.

Late industrial capitalism is out of joint with the economic imperatives of the time.[1] In the NAFTA moment, countries such

---

1. It mattered not, then, that manufacturing would be moved, more or less permanently, "offshore." Once an industry picks up stakes, it only rarely returns. It mattered not that lower labor costs in countries such as

as Mexico, China, Vietnam, and Bangladesh, represented the guarantee of lower labor costs (that is, the lowest possible labor costs), a minimal investment in the construction or maintenance of the physical plant (a plant that has proven, again and again, not only hazardous to workers' health but often fatal), no threat of unionization, no environmental legislation that could drive up costs, and, in general, a political class committed to generating national wealth through the creation (in most cases, anyway) of a manufacturing sector that had previously only been nascent but could now be expanded, exponentially, and where even criminally low wages represented an improvement in economic prospect. Offshore manufacturing was a mode of economic production that was ripe for exploitation. For the exploitation of the other.

NAFTA, economists of a certain persuasion make clear, signaled the official death knell for manufacturing in this country. To hear the likes of far-right white nationalists such as Marjorie Taylor Greene sound the "make things in America" clarion call is to know that it is, as she would insist, "antiglobalist," the surest economic sign that the "America First" movement is dedicated to that fictitious sovereign economic-political beast known as "America." It is to hear, with great apprehension, the violent white nationalism that is (at) the core of that call. Always audible, however, is the discourse of the nostalgia for late industrial capitalism. A distinct nostalgia.

Mexico, China, Indonesia, Vietnam, would be so much cheaper as to the render the US worker obscenely uncompetitive. It mattered not, then, that poor environmental laws in Pakistan and China would reduce the cost of production significantly. In the face of all of these hard economic facts, the nostalgia for late industrial capitalism persisted. As it persists today. In ever smaller pockets, ever more unable to compete against its rivals who read the economic tea leaves and took their businesses offshore, the nostalgia stages yet one more last stand.

The lost object is not Norman Rockwell's bucolic postwar New England town. It is, rather, more akin to the kind of beaten-down Rust Belt city (with its equally devastated peripheries) to which *The Deer Hunter*'s Vietnam veterans return. In other words, we're talking Clairton, Pennsylvania, just outside of Pittsburgh, where industrial decay has since the late 1960s and early 1970s become the norm. Clairton is the kind of working-class town where noncollege-educated white men are presumed to live hardscrabble but always, at least in Taylor Greene's imaginary, honorable lives. (*The Deer Hunter*'s director Michael Cimino offers a far bleaker view of the Clairtons of the world: His three returning veterans, all Slavic American, suffer not only from PTSD but also from a dislocation that is more than economically induced.) For the various Taylor Greenes who dominate our moment, loudly, Clairton is the kind of place where racial segregation is, de facto, upheld, no matter the Civil Rights movement and the legislation that ensued from it that tried to build a different America.

Cold Calling Is a Mug's Game

EVEN THAT MOST UNRELENTINGLY RUTHLESS of corporate raider movies, *Wall Street,* the other film that will figure in this essay, pays (a) tragic lip service to the ethics of American productivity. As the union man father, Carl Fox (Martin Sheen) is dropping off his son Bud (Charlie Sheen) at the New York County Courthouse, where he is about to give himself up for his role in insider trading, Carl offers this nugget of fatherly advice: "Create, instead of living off the buying and selling of others." The message is clear: earn your living through the making of something. There is, as every artisan has been instructed since time immemorial, honor in labor. This is the kind of mindset that holds itself to the standard of "job well done." To Carl Fox, his son's ambition, his desire for upward mobility, is understandable. The lack of productivity, which would appear here to be analogical to economic parasitism, is what Carl cannot abide. It is precisely Bud's inclining toward "living off the buying and selling of others" that got him to where he is: about to be charged for the crime of insider trading. At the core of Carl's admonitory advice is a form of regret that is inveterately nostalgic. Bud lost his way because he could see no value in making things. But neither was the aspirational Bud satisfied with cold calling clients at his manager's behest and offering them the opportunity for an investment that Bud promised would make his would-be clients a quick buck. Bud is wise to his manager's injunction. Cold calling is a mug's game.

Carl's dedication to building things—airplanes, in his case—suggests that late industrial capitalism, no matter its precipitous decline after its postwar dominance, also bespeaks a certain social modality. Carl has achieved his dream: the house in suburban Queens. Bud is a figure of postmodern economic ambition. Not for the son a lifetime of laboring for a single company. Not for Bud his father's suburban dream. Postmodernism, with and because of all its technological innovation, increased the speed at which life would be lived. It turned its nose up at the suburbs, it marked a renewed commitment to fast-paced urban living.

Postmodern capitalism as a mode of being is only possible, in the *Wall Street* imaginary, amidst the skyscrapers of Manhattan. It is a life that cannot be lived in a duplex in Queens. Postmodern capital would rather endure a tiny studio apartment in Manhattan than suffer the indignity of moving back into your old bedroom in your parents' house in Queens. The postmodern economy is as much about a way of life—a "lifestyle"—as it is about a relationship to rapid-fire capital accumulation. "Time is money," the motto of the postindustrial economy, means get rich quickly, and ostentatiously. It is not enough to be rich. It matters as much that your wealth be publicly visible. The aesthetic and ideological difference between old money and the arriviste class. Old money prides itself on discretion and understatement. You can tell a *parvenu* by how the labels are still, metaphorically (and maybe even literally; garishly), visible on their suit and by that gaudy Rolex on their wrist.

In the postmodern economy, to simplify the argument, it was as much a matter of how much money you made as it was a matter of how quickly you made it. The postmodern economy was an impatient beast. It would not tarry. It takes time to build things. Time that Bud did not believe he had. Bud was certainly in no mood to hang around, put in his time, and then be given a gold watch upon retirement. Bud's fate then, registers as a supreme irony. All Bud's economic impatience—his ambition—results in him "doing time."

Wall Street

FULLY AWARE THAT INDUSTRIAL CAPITALISM is yesterday's game, both films nevertheless grapple with, in a secondary register (and often in an almost incidental way), the persistence of this outmoded capitalist mode. Romantically phrased, *Wall Street* and *Pretty Woman*, as if to cinematically mark the passing of a capitalist era, pay sentimental—that is, if sentiment can be aligned with the logic of the incidental—tribute to late industrial capitalism. But if both movies register the demise of industrial capitalism, they do so in distinct registers of nostalgia. *Wall Street* is matter of fact and ruthless. That is, it is completely unsentimental about the demise of industrial capitalism, except in those moments when Carl and the wannabe yuppie Bud meet in the working-class pub that Carl and his workmates frequent. (*Yuppie*, in 1980s lexicon, was the term for a generation that understood itself as young, upwardly, socially mobile. A generation that took as its preeminent adornments fast sports cars and a Rolex, preferably a gold one.) The movie is largely lacking in sympathy for the union-man's son, the "NYU Business School" graduate who is caught out by the Securities and Exchange Commission (SEC) and will have to serve prison time for his role in insider trading; the son who could not resist the wiles and temptations—the financial perks, the chance to move out of his tiny Manhattan studio, the women—made immanent for him by Gordon Gekko, *the* poster boy for1980s corporate raider capitalism. Gekko is a character that is said to have been modeled on, appropriate for the zeitgeist of the 1980s, Michael Milken (the master broker of worthless high-yield bonds, that is, "junk bonds," for which Milken would be imprisoned) and Stone himself—Stone's father was a Wall Street stockbroker during the Great Depression and the movie is a tribute to Lou Stone.

Even as Bud Fox gets ready to face jail time for his "insider training," *Wall Street* remains unrepentant about the exploitative destruction that corporate raider capitalism visits upon industrial capitalism. No surprise, since the movie is an ode to Gekko's infamous motto: "Greed is good." Words to live by, and, as such, also words to die by. "Greed is good" stands as an unsentimental, rude obituary to industrial capitalism. Wall Street greed is how industrial capitalism meets its rough end.

And who better to issue that death certificate than Gordon Gekko, that most ruthless of corporate raiders. Our Mr. Gecko is a study in corporate raider capitalist self-confidence, a self-confidence, however, that derives from a bitter lower-middle-class consciousness. A "City College" graduate, Gekko, his hair is slicked back just so, his high-end suspenders holding up his immaculately tailored pinstripe suits, with matching French-collar shirts and boutique neckties, is in the business of not only accumulating obscene amounts of money. He is also getting his revenge on those "Yale and Harvard boys." *Wall Street* is what happens when the lower middle class, unapologetic about its desire for capital accumulation, uses its street smarts to game the system. And we can say that, in beating the financial system, it also reveals the bankruptcy that is at the core of global finance. The system is always only one hustle away from being ruthlessly exposed.

As in the case of the French Revolution, when the maritime bourgeoisie found the discrepancy between their vast riches and their middling class standing intolerable, class warfare is always waged most intensely by those who have the most to gain. Those who have the most to gain at the expense of those who for too long, in the minds of this particular constituency within the historically excluded (the maritime bourgeoisie; the colonized elite; and various other stripes of the *parvenu*), have kept them out. Those who have denied the historically excluded their fair share of the economic pie. Even though he has managed, for the price of a mere one million dollars, to secure himself a seat on the board of the Bronx Zoo, Gekko still burns with class rage, as a consequence of which he wages his own private class warfare from within the plush environs of his spacious office, with at least three brokers present to do his bidding, to execute his wishes.

Carl, who belongs, roughly, to the same generation as Gekko, instantiates a very different set of values (virtues?). Carl Fox belongs to a white American middle class that is satisfied with a modest home in the outer New York City borough of Queens, the house to which Bud cannot return. Carl regards the working man who pays his union dues as a respectable citizen because he has made something of his life. Carl provides for his family, so much so that he can afford to loan his wannabe yuppie son the odd $200 or $300 when Bud is in a pinch. Such home comforts are scorned by Gekko. In fact, making such a pact with life registers as failure to Gekko. No matter that Carl has put his son through college and stands his son a beer, "a Molson Lite," while ordering a helping of "spaghetti" at his local bar. This humdrum respectable life is not that to which a City College graduate aspires, certainly not one who is full of animus toward the Ivy Leaguers who consider themselves his social superiors.

His social superiors, maybe, but in every social encounter with them we see the Ivy League types obsequiously trying to curry favor with this nouveau riche corporate raider. Gekko responds by either backslapping or insulting them.

You Are the Suit You Wear

SARTORIAL EXEMPLARITY is a matter of importance to Gekko. "Don't come in here again dressed like that," Gekko reprimands Bud at their first lunch meeting. No Wall Street broker who reports to and keeps company with Gordon Gekko would deign to wear *prêt-à-porter*. To rectify matters sartorial, Gekko gives Bud the name of his tailor. Gekko does not explicitly warn Bud against his penchant for Brooks Brothers button downs and rep ties, but the sartorial injunction is clear. "Get thee to my tailor:" learn to dress as I do.

Meanwhile, Gekko is quietly locked into his own sartorial standoff, one that is international in its reverberations and not at all local.

If Bud Fox is a young man of ambition caught between two worlds, Carl's and Gekko's, if Bud is trying to negotiate between two sets of opposing values (the union man in his overalls and the corporate raider), if Bud is in the process of ditching his $400 *prêt-à-porter* attire for Gekko-like bespoke suits, then Gekko is not only matching his financial muscle with but also pitting his sartorial wits against his English corporate raider counterpart: Sir Lawrence Wildman (Terence Stamp), who here represents that most famous of English corporate raiders, Sir James Goldsmith. "Sir Larry" is a study in Saville Row understatement. Tasteful, sober, Prince of Wales checks, cutaway collars, Windsor knotted ties.

This is the ultimate sartorial transatlantic showdown. American flash versus the timeless and enduring elegance of the Olde World. Like his clothing, Gekko is front and center, the camera attending to his attire in concentrated wide shots, as if to capture the full impact of its allure. Sir Larry appears almost always in profile. As if we are only meant to catch a glimpse of the richness of the fabric of his suit, as if that is enough to settle the sartorial matter in the Englishman's favor. Turns out that a bold blue woolen chalk stripe suit may be able to hide a multitude of moral failings, but it can't swing the sartorial battle in the American's favor. Less, as they say, is more. Score one for the Olde World. "Greed" may be "good," and Sir Larry may find himself outsmarted by his hungrier and more unscrupulous (it's a matter of degree, not a difference in type) American corporate raider counterpart, but his understatement wins the day, at least sartorially.

Raymond Williams: A Brief Word

SON OF THE WELSH BORDERLANDS, lifelong—third generation, at that—Labour Party member, was Raymond Williams. He was that literary critic who always located the production of literature in its historical moment, attentive always to the conditions that made the literary artifact possible, that shaped it, that gave the literary its "structure of feeling," a phrase for which he is perhaps most famous.

But Williams was by no means a literary man only. Far from it, as his work in *Culture & Society* makes evident. No surprise, then, that in the course of his critiques Williams developed a tripartite understanding of ideology. He offered three categories, explicating how one ideology was never quite singular. It contained, the ideology of the day, three distinct articulations: dominant, emergent, and residual. The emergent is that which is (already) lodged within the dominant but has not yet risen to prominence; the dominant is self-explanatory. What preoccupies us here is the residual: it is that mode of being (those "structures of feeling," those economic modes, those political ideologies, those social mores, and so on) that is still operative in the dominant but only as the remnant of the previous dispensation.

The residual ideology, sedimented within the dominant, can be absorbed into the dominant because it no longer threatens the dominant. It can, if truth be told, be useful to the dominant ideology to retain within itself traces of its antecedent. Perhaps even antecedents. Broadly speaking, Marx and Williams are aligned in their thinking on the transition from one mode of production to another and are, as is obvious, ideologically aligned in their critique of the immanent effects of capitalism on the human experience, to say nothing of the costs it exacts on the human psyche. If Marx's critique tends more toward a discourse of exhaustion, an economic mode can only be replaced when the mode that preceded it has been thoroughly exploited, Marx and Williams converge around the emergent. Marx's metaphor of incipient maternal (re)production, "the womb of the old," finds its corollary in Williams's category of the emergent. (Williams's thinking, we can say, turns on the possibility of the trace; the trace as residue—containing within it that which, chronologically speaking, belongs to the past—and the trace as germ—the trace *l'avenir,* the present containing within it the—economic—mode to come.) In *Pretty Woman,* Marx and Williams's critiques find reinforcement in each other even as we acknowledge that there is a useful precision in Williams's terminology.

Following Williams, then, we can name late industrial capitalism "residual." However, we can do so only if we keep in mind that the imperative(s) of postindustrial capital is singular. Unlike Williams's dominant ideology, postindustrial capital will not tolerate the residual to persist in any way into its era, a tension to which Marx's critique would appear to be sensitive. The residual mode of economic production must be, not to put too fine a point on it, liquidated. The only purpose of the residual, insofar as it still exists (despite postindustrial capitalism's ongoing efforts to render it obsolete), is instrumental. Whatever value resides in it must be exploited to the full.

Unlike Williams's dominant ideology, postindustrial capital is ruthless. It has no time for that which preceded it. Having outmoded industrialism, postindustrial capital refuses to absorb the residual into itself. Succinctly phrased, postindustrial capital is brutally unsentimental. The past must be abandoned to itself. Not a single trace of it must be allowed to remain. If nostalgia cannot return a profit, what value has it? None.

But then, ruthless though its logic be, what postindustrial capital had not reckoned with is a singular cinematic force: a pretty woman. A pretty woman who uses her body to make a living and, as such, it is unsurprising that she will take her cues from the labor modality of late industrial capitalism. (In fairness to the history of the prostitute, however, we should recognize that the basic tools of her profession have changed very little since time immemorial.) The working body, what postindustrial capital takes to be, in the age of private equity finance, a relic, maybe even an economic dinosaur.

In *Pretty Woman* we encounter an old man, James Morse (Ralph Bellamy, in his final performance) who still clings to his truth.[1] That it remains possible to "Make things in America." James Morse is a retiring ship builder who is refusing to sell his company to Edward Lewis unless it continues to be productive, under the terms of his residual economic rubric. James Morse is accompanied by his grandson, David (Alex Hyde-White). (There is no mention of David's father, so we are free to speculate that he has either passed on or figures as the missing generation. Have we found in the absent father that male family member who has succumbed to the logic of postindustrial capital and has abandoned the family business?)

---

1. To borrow a term from Jean-Paul Sartre in his biography of Jean Genet, James Morse is a "*passéistes*," a man "not adapted to the present age, who is not a man of his time, who 'lives in the past.'" Sartre, *Saint Genet: Actor and Martyr,* trans. Bernard Frechtman (New York: George Braziller, 1963), 1.

What we have, then, is an unlikely triumvirate of actors who are making this last stand against postindustrial capital. (Grand) father, (grand) son, and woman of the streets. And alongside this trio a smooth, suave PEF who is surprisingly open to—maybe even sentimental about—the prospect of accommodating one of the last scions of late industrial capitalism.

A case of postindustrial Goliath going up against late industrial David. Hardly a fair fight, one would imagine.

Still, stay tuned. After all, as the neighborhood crier hollers into the blankness of the day at the end of the movie, "This is Hollywood, where all your dreams come true!" Especially dreams condemned to the dustbin of history decades ago.

The Patient Is on Life Support but Is Not Yet Dead

GORDON GEKKO IS A STREET FIGHTER, an alleyway financial brawler in an expensive suit. *Pretty Woman* presents James Morse as an old-schooled, buttoned-down, but tough-as-nails industrial capitalist. If Bud Fox is no match for Gekko, then what James and David Morse find in Edward is a PEF who is, if not possessed of a conscience lately come by exactly, then a postindustrial capitalist who, at the very last second, it seems, decides to check on the ever-weakening pulse of industrial capitalism.

The verdict is peremptory but not inconsequential. American late industrial capitalism is on life support. Every now and then—and it does not matter if we're talking about the early 1990s or the third decade of the twenty-first century—the patient blinks. Or the patient, ailing and almost beyond economic recognition, reaches out a feeble hand, just enough to suggest that it still has a pulse. The occasional call for the revitalization of the American manufacturing industry is that speaking, with a regularity that should not surprise us but nonetheless always does, of an economic nationalism that can always be brought to life. Especially in those moments when the United States fears that its global dominance is under threat.

It is, of course, in precisely those moments when the racism and xenophobia that are so constitutive of this economic nationalism are mobilized, sometimes subtly, sometimes less so (as in the current battle for global dominance with China). Economic nostalgia is always embedded within the American political.

The PEF's decision to keep building ships submits, as befits the movie's romantic thematic, to a strain of nostalgia. As such, the desire to resuscitate late industrial capitalism operates as a secondary discourse in *Pretty Woman*. The determination to "make something in America" (to "make things in America again") is the story that suffuses the movie's main plot—the redemption of the wanton, destructive venture capitalism by the prostitute. It might even be more appropriate to say that *Pretty Woman* functions in a redemptive Christological register in that it stands as the desire for the resurrection of industrial capitalism, against all hard economic evidence that declares this mode of capitalism dead; or at the very least, that industrial capitalism has for decades been surpassed as the dominant capitalist mode of producing—reproducing—wealth. (Industrial capitalism will not, some three decades after its heyday, unlike Jesus the Christ, rise again on the third day.)

However, thinking late/industrial capitalism's deep attachment to its outmoded modality, which also serves as a shorthand for its motto, "Make things in America, again," resonates in a distinctly different timbre in a post-2016 America. The 1990 economic nationalism of *Pretty Woman,* in which were always incubating the seeds of a white nationalism potentially virulent in its xenophobia, in which could always be detected the strains of a white racism angry at the (largely) meager economic gains made by black Americans and other minorities, can be said to have come fully into itself since 2016.

The Baseness of/in the Superstructure

"MAKING THINGS IN AMERICA" has matured, at least ideologically. That is, it has mutated into the political monster, it has become that political animal that is unapologetic and historically retrograde in its racism (the African American Manhattan District Attorney Alvin Bragg, who prosecuted the Stormy Daniels case, is "an animal," once more evoking the bestiality that is blackness),[1] militantly misogynistic (the porn star Stormy Daniels, whom Trump tried to pay off, is a "horseface"), and unrestrained in its xenophobia (the pandemic as the "China virus"; nations in the Caribbean and Africa denounced as "shthole countries").

"Make American Great Again" (MAGA) might not be exactly the monstrous adult love child of "Making things in America" (MTIA) and nostalgia for industrial capitalism, but there is no doubting the toxic ideological intimacy of the relationship between these two modes of American economic *poesis*. If, as Marx

---

1. To which we might add the names of New York State Attorney General Letitia James and the Fulton County, Georgia, District Attorney Fani Willis.

insists, the superstructure always follows the base, then we can say that *Pretty Woman* inverts this model. It is the superstructure that stands as an instance of the cinematic as economic prescience.

MTIA has found its mutant ideological maturation in MAGA. Or better to say that MTIA has revealed its ideological truth in/ as MAGA. Teleologically phrased, you are what you become. In this way, Hollywood offered us, without knowing it, a foretaste of what the discourse of "Making things in America" was to become. The non-college-educated white male forms the base constituency for the nostalgia for late industrial capitalism, driving the ideological vituperation that is the MAGA movement. The baseness of this ideological call has proven itself historically successful precisely because it does not submit to the logic of sophisticated economic analysis. Or, for that matter, any economic analysis that does not reaffirm the return of the manufacturing base. (A matter of will, this return; not economics truth) The MTIA's ideological call will not abide the complicity of the US trade union movement in the NAFTA agreement. Nor will it countenance a critique of why it is possible to buy so many "Made in China/Vietnam/Cambodia" goods cheaply at Walmart or any of those other big-box stores. Exploitation of the other is always permissible under the sign of erasure—it is, as Marx would have it, reification in its purest form. The ideology that is MTIA or MAGA succeeds because of its direct address to the nostalgia for that mythical era, a moment that always, in one way or another, turns on the postwar boom that was the 1950s, that moment that was Yankee economic nationalism, a moment that cannot be disarticulated from the ideological and economic aggression that was US neo-imperialism.

Much of the political potency—its mobilizing potentiality— of MTIA and MAGA must be attributed to its capacity to articulate itself as an ideology determined to return to that moment when the nation was an unchallenged global (economic) force. That is—and this is perhaps more obvious in the case of Thatcherism—it is a nostalgia for imperial greatness. In Thatcher's jingoistic terms, "Put the Great Back in Great Britain." For Reagan it functioned similarly, but the sting of defeat was sharper in the case of the United States: the loss incurred in Vietnam, the specter of body bags returning from the war in southeast Asia, the inability to resolve the Iran hostage crisis, to say nothing of the racial violence of the late-1960s Newark, Detroit, Oakland. All these national and international catastrophes weighed heavily on the American psyche. Hence Reagan's own Biblical jingoism, the promise of America once more as that "shining city on a hill." "It's a new day in America;" "It's morning in America," Reagan intoned, repeatedly. Implicit in Reagan's Christological promise of ideological redemption and economic rebirth was the desire for the return of the United States to the status of global hegemon. At the very core of every hegemon is the dream of eternal rule, a dream most poetically rendered by imperial Britain: "The sun will never set on the British Empire."

Nostalgia for the industrial economic base (and lament for the erosion of the US manufacturing base) amounts to what we might term the loss an onto-economic self. The de-basing of that base must, according to Marx, find its articulation in the superstructure. And what could be more glamorously superstructural than a Hollywood movie that represents the nostalgia for that loss? *Pretty Woman* is a cinematic mourning for an ideologically beloved mode of being, of being a white, non-college-educated male in America. Surely hell hath no fury like a white, non-college-educated male superannuated by the export of the US manufacturing base to China, *communist* China, of all places? Who cares about the ideological—which is to say, economic—complexities ushered in by Deng Xiaoping's own version of state capitalism? A degraded economic base, we can say, will reflect itself in/as an ideologically abhorrent superstructure.

Out of MTIA the political vituperation that is Trumpism will find its political ideology will only become more violent in its odiousness as the MAGA base finds itself ever more the self-proclaimed victims of "globalism" as technological advances—AI, to cite just the most obvious example—render greater numbers of the work force superfluous. What is the MAGA base *to do,* how will this base provide for its alimentary needs, as the future presents itself as nothing but the bleak possibility of long-term unemployment or, at best, menial labor? Or, even worse, to be reduced to the prospect of seasonal labor. If seasonal labor comes to represent their only economic prospect, will it then only be the antebellum "aristocracy of the skin" that distinguishes MAGA loyalists from those they, in their xenophobia, so despise? "Illegal immigrants?"

It is, therefore, not in the least paradoxical that Margorie Taylor Greene, among the most vehement of the MTIA spokes-persons, represents a northwestern Georgia district that is pre-dominantly rural. (Georgia's 14th district, bordered to the north by Tennessee and to the west by Alabama, also has an exurban constituency.) In the concatenation of MTIA to MAGA, it does not matter that the constituents you represent are themselves the "victims" of America's manufacturing de-basement. All that is of consequence is that the discourse of "America First," which is probably where the MTIA-MAGA ideological trajectories con-join, figures prominently as a rhetorical device.

In the MTIA-MAGA-America-First universe, then, no politics is local. Instead, it is the spirit of the times—nostalgia, as a re-gressive articulation—that must be captured, that must be kept alive in the public sphere. The effect of this tripartite ideological alliance is that it guarantees that there will, in our moment and in every moment to come, be a future for nostalgia.

There will always be rhetorical work for nostalgia. Nostalgia as definitively inexhaustible. Nostalgia as infinite mourning for the irretrievable object—the past.

It is, then, never a matter of *who* is enfranchised to speak it. It matters only *that* nostalgia is kept in good ideological health. That it is conscripted into regular rhetorical duty. It is not, as Taylor Greene's pronouncements make clear, *who* but *what* you represent.

Working Women

The burnt-out ends of smoky days.

—T. S. ELIOT, "Preludes"

WHAT IS REPRESENTED by the MTIA-MAGA-America First discourse is the impossible promise to retrieve the unretrievable. The *poesis* of a nostalgia constructed out of the ruin of late industrial capitalism, a ruin such as only PEF can make out of industrial capitalism. A ruin that bears within it the traces of a labor force ruined by PEF.

A rhetoric composed of ideological fragments and stray ends selectively stitched together out of the economic devastation borne by human beings now thrown aimlessly adrift in that debased manufacturing world. Schumpeter's "creative destruction," Eliot's "burnt-out ends of smoky days." Such a ruin that James Morse will avoid, at least temporarily, but that remains economically inexorable because all we can excavate from the ruin that is industrial capitalism is what we already expect to find. Eliot's poem comes quickly to mind, again, because it lays before us as a moment of splendidly desolate destruction; "Preludes" as an unsentimental testament to modernist conformity and ennui.

Eliot's metaphor made all the more grim by an industrial pollution that hangs like a pall over the inscape of his poem.

Who can labor under such a pall? What can the working man produce in this degraded air? And what of the working woman, hardly a type with which Eliot is overly familiar and certainly not a type who occupies him in his oeuvre? Nevertheless, Eliot gives us just such a figure. Trapped in a dingy apartment, a woman—white, no doubt—of the English lower classes, a woman on the verge of physical ruin:

> You had such a vision of the street
> As the street hardly understands;
> Sitting along the bed's edge, where
> You curled the papers from your hair,
> Or clasped the yellow soles of feet
> In the palms of both soiled hands.[1]

How is the world to be held in such "soiled hands?"

Or, it may be that only if the PEF world is held in hands deemed ethically "soiled" that the advance of finance capital can be stayed. Vulture capitalism, of the *Wall Street* variety, can only be thwarted with hands that know, intimately, the place of labor in the history of capital. Only the woman who works (walks) the streets for a living could possibly know the streets, can even hope to have "such a vision of the street / As the street hardly understands."

While we could say that the economy of the street depends on its own triangulated hierarchy (pimps ↔ prostitute ↔ johns), the greater majority of that economy is transacted not vertically but horizontally. The johns pay the pimps, hand to hand, the hookers

---

1. T. S. Eliot, *Collected Poems 1902–1962* (Faber & Faber, 1983), 23.

get their money from their pimps. Hand-to-hand exchanges, to say nothing of that stock-in-trade use of the prostitute's hand.

All that remains from these exchanges is paper (money) and the transmission of bodily fluids. On the one hand, there would appear to be not a lot to "understand" about the "street." On the other, how can we tally with any precision just how much needs to be "understood" about the "street," everything that has to be seen in order to transact, survive, and if at all possible (should the prostitute or the pimp so decide) to extricate the self from the "street."

What is the effect, as Randy Crawford sings in 1987 (fronting The Crusaders, a jazz trio), of living a "street" as a life sentence. To not be able to live life off the streets. To know the "street" as erasing any sustainable difference between life and death. In a boppy voice, just barely tinged with regret, Crawford sings,

> I play the streetlife, because there's no place I can go
> Streetlife, it's the only life I know
> Streetlife, and there's a thousand parts to play
> Streetlife, until you play your life away
> The prostitute, dead in a dumpster.
> "Streetlife, for a nickel or a dime."[2]

Homicide, life on the streets.

There are hints, and not, on the face of it, subtle ones, that there is reason for ethical caution around the working woman of Eliot's poem. Her profession may be an aged one. The oldest one, as we are wont to say: "You had such a vision of the street / As the street hardly understands" is as close to calling a woman

---

2. "Street Life," lyrics by Randy Crawford, in The Crusaders, *Street Life* (MCA Records, 1979).

a prostitute—directly, that is; there are other poems where his allusions are more middlebrow—as Eliot ever gets.

However, where Eliot hedges his bets ever so slightly, *Pretty Woman* pulls no punches. Vivian is a prostitute stereotypical in her self-presentation—cheap wig, short skirt, heavily made-up, always chewing gum. Vivian is nonetheless very attractive, worthy of being paid tribute by the warbling voice of Roy Orbison, the writer of the song from which Marshall's movie takes its name. Vivian, by all accounts, is very good at her chosen profession.

Late Industrial Capitalism 1:
"Making Things in America"

TO PROPOSE THAT there is such a phenomenon as late industrial capitalism is, of course, to break with the conventional
chronology of capitalist development. Schematically rendered:
feudalism ↔ industrialism (the first stage in the invention of
machinery that reorganizes human labor, and, indeed, human
life, completely disrupting life as previously lived) ↔ increased
mechanization, greater efficiency (Taylorism, the assembly line,
increased mass production; post–World War II, the creation of
mass consumerism) ↔ postindustrial capitalism / late capitalism
(the decline of manufacturing, replaced by a service economy
and the rise of finance capital). One of the defining features of
late capitalism, as Fredric Jameson has long since instructed us,[1]
is that it makes of everything a commodity—not only material
resources but *everything,* including, saliently, the aesthetic: art,
culture, the media, advertising, and so on—to say nothing of the
ways in which postmodern capitalism technologically dominates

1. Fredric Jameson, *Postmodernism, or, The Cultural Logic of Late
Capitalism* (Duke University Press, 1999).

our age.[2] The shocking effect of late capitalism, as elucidated by Jameson in his critique of Ernst Mandel's *Late Capitalism,* is that it is showing itself to be the "purest form of capital yet to have emerged, a prodigious expansion of capital into hitherto uncommodified areas."[3]

So pure a form of capital will brook no residualism. Those economic modes that are incompatible with late industrial capitalism will no longer, Jameson writes, be allowed to endure: "This purer capitalism of our own time thus eliminates the enclaves of precapitalist organization it had hitherto tolerated and exploited in a tributary way."[4] If the logic of Mandel's chronology of capitalism is the dialectic, and as such can "tolerate" the residual (the dominant mode of capital production can abide—accommodate and coexist with—older modes of production, as long as that mode does not threaten it as an economic practice), then the logic of late capitalism is more consistent with the spirit at of Thomas Hobbes's *Leviathan*—all residuals will be eliminated in a fashion that will surely be "nasty and brutish." In place of the dialectic comes an absolute rupture: the complete severing of the new, surging, mode of capital from its predecessor, a predecessor made obsolete and redundant by this new insurgent named late capitalism.

2. Engaging, and in so doing extending Jameson's argument in *Postmodernism,* Jeffrey Nealon names our moment, or one that is just past—or passing, even—*Post-postmodernism: Or, the Cultural Logic of Just-in-Time Capitalism* (Stanford University Press, 2012).

3. Jameson, *Postmodernism,* 36.

4. Jameson, 36.

Late Industrial Capitalism 2: Nostalgia and Grievance

EDWARD LEWIS is in the business of buying up "distressed companies." The reason, in Lewis's predatory logic, these companies are in financial distress is that they are anachronistic. This point is driven home to Edward relentlessly by his henchman Philip Stuckey, an unscrupulous postindustrial capitalist. Or, we might say, the *most* scrupulous postindustrial capitalist because he is totally immune to nostalgia. Stuckey is in no way sentimental about the demise of American manufacturing or anything that smacks of the residual. Edward and Stuckey belong to the era before, as Jameson would say, capital became relentlessly "pure." That moment when capital still "tolerated" modes of production incommensurate with itself.

Late industrial capitalism is the plaintive cry emanating from an already destroyed mode of economic production. Late industrial capitalism is, as such, unscientific, a ruined mode of production that is already antiquated and will soon meet the fate of obsolescence it so richly deserves. And we know that Marx set great store by the science of capitalism. Late industrial capital insists that, all evidence to the contrary, it is still possible to "make things in America," that a devastated manufacturing base, if it is left unmolested by PEF, can be resuscitated. In some places, at least. In some industries, surely. That the dignity of honest white labor can be restored, all economic trends and indicators to the contrary.

"Making things in America" as innately ideological, the perpetration of an economic false consciousness on that constituency— white workers (intensely masculinized)—most receptive to it. Those for whom "globalization" resonates as a historic grievance, as economic evidence that it is the Other who is "stealing jobs from Americans." The politics of grievance brought to a new pitch of intensity by a wealthy white speculator—hotelier, global land speculator (in the United States, Asia, Europe), failed Atlantic City casino mogul—who has never handled a piece of machinery in his life. No matter; this politician was skilled enough in the cynical ability to turn the politics of white grievance into a potent form of political capital that it catapulted him right into the White House. Such is the power of perceived injury, a power mobilized with injurious consequences for the Other.

A singular form of economic conversion this is: the ability to meld economic nostalgia with white political grievance and to make out of this blend a resonant, volatile, nationalist ideological cocktail. "Making things in America" resonates because it diverts attention from the hard economic truths of postindustrial capital. If nostalgia cannot be assigned an economic value, the ideology of white *ressentiment* is, politically, at least, measurable. It translates into votes. The articulation of nostalgia makes of the discourse of nostalgia itself the cathected object. Nostalgia becomes the Kantian thing in itself: *das Ding an sich*.

On Morality: A Brief Žižekian Word

THE LOGIC OF CONSUMER CAPITAL IS, in Žižek's terms, immoral. Žižek's distinction between morality and ethics, for all its geometric pretenses, evinces an unmistakably Christian mode of being in the world: "Morality is concerned with the symmetry of my relations with other human beings; its zero-level rule is 'do not do to me what you do not want me to do to you'; ethics, on the contrary, deal with my consistency with myself, my fidelity to my own desires."[1] "Do unto others as you would have them do unto you" is how I recall it. (In the terms of the King James Bible, Matthew 7:12: "Therefore all things whatsoever ye would that men should do to you, do ye even so to them: for this is the law and the prophets.") The effect of moral "symmetry," then, is that Action I, because it is equal to Action II (I = II; II = I), prevents any aberrant (unfair, unjust) behavior. (This is morality as Newtonian science, as least as it pertains to Newton's Third Law of Motion: every action has an equal and opposite reaction. Morality secures "equilibrium" between actors. Or, as a deterrent, the Cold War logic of mutually assured destruction.)

1. Slavoj Žižek, *In Defense of Lost Causes* (Verso, 2008), 223.

It is its inherent "asymmetry" that makes of postindustrial capital an "immoral" force: the refusal to "do unto the Other as you have the Other do unto you"; that is, not insisting that there should be the universal imposition of fair labor practices, which include the outlawing of child labor, that environmental standards should be globally enforced, that the health and safety of all workers must be protected.

It's Big in Japan

LATE INDUSTRIAL CAPITALIST NOSTALGIA is what happens when the dialectic dies, is put to death because PEF has determined that there is no value in its existence. In fact, its only value is what can be attained through the selling off of manufacturing's remaining assets. What does not yield value—that is, cannot return a profit, cannot be turned into a profit—is to be disposed of with all due haste.

Asset stripping is the complete opposite of industrialized production. It takes the prostitute to make immanent to the PEFs (Stuckey more than Edward) the logic of late industrial capitalism. More than that, it is the despoiled woman who becomes the spokesperson for a (US) fin-de-siècle late industrial capitalism reduced to bare bones, the US industrial economy for which James Morse wants to assure a future has been, in Édouard Glissant's critique of the various forms of colonial extraction, "stripped to essentials."[1]

To "strip" assets, in the discourse of late-twentieth-century capitalism, is to hew to the logic of the corporate raider, the vulture capitalist, one such as Edward who, in the clearest pos-

---

1. Édouard Glissant, *Caribbean Discourse: Selected Essays*, trans. Michael Dash (University of Virginia Press, 1999), 50.

sible terms, explains his practice to Vivian. He starts out, "I buy companies that are in financial distress," after which he proceeds to treat Vivian with a quick, gentlemanly, "Warn me if I bore you," to the basic, and therefore most felicitous, course in vulture capitalism:

> Twenty years ago Morse Industries was a huge corporation, and even though they're almost bankrupt today, they still have millions in assets. Real estate, equipment, inventory. Things that can be liquidated to generate cash. You understand?

Morse Industries has been in the shipbuilding business for forty years, during which it has acquired a swathe of property, which are the floundering company's most valuable assets. Stuckey, the point man on the deal, has done his job thoroughly. In his PowerPoint presentation, Stuckey lays out the plan for acquisition:

> This is the jewel in Morse's crown. Prime industrial property straddling the Port of Long Beach and Los Angeles. We can strip out all the heavy equipment. Some of the cranes are very valuable overseas. World War II stuff that nobody builds anymore because it costs too much. The Japanese are salivating for them.

In the past Morse Industries built destroyers for the US Navy, a business that included providing ships for the Navy during World War II. The logic of PEF is ruthless, completely free of sentiment. Where Stuckey sees disposable machinery—"Some of the cranes are very valuable overseas"—others see the potential for "creation" out of this capitalist "destruction." "The Japanese are salivating for them," Stuckey says, almost chuckling at the prospect of offloading Morse Industries vital machinery for a quick buck. But "these cranes" have acquired, in being brought to historical life again, an ideological resonance. The "cranes" evoke, as they must, a history of catastrophic, world-altering violence.

The *Boro* Aesthetic

THE JAPANESE, in the high moment of neoliberal capitalism that was the 1980s through the 1990s, emerged as a dominant economic force on the world market and were the precursors to the rise of the Asian Tiger economies. The four nations that comprised the Asian Tigers, Hong Kong, South Korea, Taiwan, and Singapore, became economically prosperous because, starting in the 1960s at the very moment that manufacturing was declining the West, they rapidly industrialized, as well as developing a prosperous export economy.

That the Japanese are, at least in Stuckey's account, "salivating" at the prospect of buying up the kind of machinery that was at optimal performance in the 1940s, has the effect of confronting us with a historic event. That Japanese industry is "salivating" at being able to acquire Morse Industries' machinery does not mark a simple return to (although, as we know, there is no such thing as an uncomplicated turning-back-to; nostalgia is a complex phenomenon) nor the blind determination to turn away from a historic catastrophe; it marks, rather, the return of the event that was nuclear disaster—Hiroshima and Nagasaki. In the light of what the Morse Industries cranes (the "relic" of the industrial era) reanimates, the memory of death that it brings once again to life, Stuckey's bland assertion—"it costs too much"—assumes a meaning entirely beyond the range of his, or, for that matter, postindustrial capital's, thinking.

Stuckey's easy dismissal of a mode of production that was historically vital in the Allied victory over the Axis powers takes on a far more cynical and historically sinister meaning. How are we to assign value to the lives destroyed in that war, to the planetary destruction visited upon the people of the region, the effects of which continue to be felt today in Japan? Can we put a number on that? Or, in terms of costs, what are we to make Robert Oppenheimer's regret about his signal role in the creation of the A-Bomb? How are we to ever stop looking on those ruins? The "burnt-out ends of a smoky day" that will not end? The "burnt-out ends of *the* smoky day" of all "smoky days?" A "smoky day" that had about it the distinct prospect of being an "end day?" *The end day to end all days.*

At the very least, we know that the ruin that is the toxic aftermath of Hiroshima and Nagasaki must always be looked upon, must be turned to, especially in those moments when it appears to be slipping from our immediate view; that moment when it is no longer located at forefront of our thinking. But the machinic, economic ruin(s) that have nothing but disposable economic value to Stuckey (and to Edward, too) ignores the creativity that emanated from that violent ruin—the defeat of Japan in 1945. In the wake of that defeat, in light of that ecological horror, in the aftermath of an economy left in tatters by war, the Japanese set about rebuilding their economy. And, in at least one way, the Japanese produced their own creativity out of the ruins of ideological, economic, and political destruction.

Even before that moment when the Japanese economy, especially through electronics and the production of fuel-efficient cars, was coming to global prominence, a singular aesthetic emerged in the world of Japanese fashion. Even before the coming to prominence of that couture aesthetic we know today as *boro* culture, there was a signal stirring on the Japanese fashion front.

W. David Marx, a Japanese-based American critic of Japanese fashion, describes the scarcity of material with which to make new clothes in postwar Japan. The "postwar government," Marx writes,

> campaigned for frugality and moderation. Between the U.S. stopping all commercial imports of textiles and garments to Japan and a rationing system set up in 1947, few could buy or even make new clothing. The only fresh source of shirts and pants came from boxes of used garments collected in American charity drives, most of which ended up in the black markets.[1]

In an economy where new raw materials were at a premium, the Japanese returned to an earlier mode of cloth making, what we know today as *boro* clothing or *boro* culture, as some might prefer. *Boro* culture is, arguably, best apprehended as the art of *making-do* with what is at hand. As we know from W. David Marx, the Japanese clothing industry was without access to reams of new cloth, thanks to the "U.S. stopping all commercial imports of textiles and garments to Japan." Out of resilience as much as the hard truth of having no alternative, the Japanese clothing industry made do with scraps of old cloth, the remnants of old bales of wool, cutting up old garments (some of them no doubt acquired on the "black market") to either repurpose them or to make entirely new garments.

Distinct about the turn to *boro* culture was its obsession with "Ivy League" American fashion, what W. David Marx presents as—and takes as the title of his book—"*Ametora,* the Japanese

---

1. W. David Marx's *Ametora: How Japan Saved American Style* (Basic Books, 2015), 11.

slang abbreviation of 'American traditional.'"[2] Equally resonant, in the terms of our argument, is that this turn to America as a model for postwar fashion was that—especially salient in a culture as patriarchal as Japan's—its first practitioners were neither men nor "respectable" Japanese women. Instead, it was the "Pan Pan girls": "Prewar, Western fashion and custom had entered society through the male elite and trickled down. In a topsy-turvy social reversal, the first to wear American-style clothing in postwar Japan were women—and prostitutes at that."[3] The "Pan Pan girls" "wore brightly colored American dresses and platform heels, with a signature kerchief tied around their necks. They permed their hair, caked on heavy makeup, and wore red lipstick and red nail polish."[4] Vivian in Tokyo, circa 1948. With a miniskirt instead of a "brightly colored dress," with no "caked on heavy makeup," and with those "platform heels" replaced by stilettos. But never quite giving up on the dream of the glorious cocktail dress fit for that upscale polo game where PEFs conduct their business while the riders battle it out on their ponies. Edward can, for example, at a polo match pretty much close a deal or instruct Stuckey to get a senator on the phone to stymie a competitor's efforts to remain solvent.

At first, this mode of clothes-making was regarded as a historical necessity. And, because *boro* culture recalled a moment before Japan's rise as an imperial power and then, in the wake of the war, its rapid industrialization, it was frowned upon, mostly because it was a reminder of the nation's military defeat. However, from the 1980s through 2000, with the founding of companies such as "Engineered Garments" (Daiki Suzuki, founder of the fashion empire that is Nepenthes; a brand known as "EG" to

2. Marx, xvi.
3. Marx, 12.
4. Marx, 12.

its loyalists), "Beams +" (Hideki Mizobata), "orSlow" (Ichiro Nakatsu), "Visvim" (Hiroki Nakamura, founded in 2000), and, my favorite, Kapital (founded in 1984 by Toshikiyo Hirata, who now works together with his son, Kiro, in Okayama, Japan's denim capital), *boro* culture became a hot fashion item. Kapital, orSlow, Visvim are now among the go-to brands for hipsters the world over.[5]

Even as *boro* has evolved into a distinctly Japanese and internationally celebrated mode of fashion, it remains unabashed in its appropriation of US culture. The foundation of this aesthetic is, as we said, American preppy. For *boro* culture, Yale is the go-to Ivy League model. So, think postwar Ivy League,[6] button-down

5. *Boro* culture is, of course, not limited to Japan. Not only has it influenced US fashion (a case a return to the "original" that can no longer stake the claim to being "original" in a form at once recognizable and dissonant) but *boro* culture has made its mark in countries such as South Korea (Eastlogue, which is based on the same US preppy and military culture; but Eastlogue is not quite as "street" as, say, Kapital) and France (where brands such as A.P.C. Ami and Arpenteur clearly belong to the same genus). Here mention must be made of the influential Japanese designer Kenzo Takada, who was based in Paris but first made his mark in his native Japan. Kenzo, now under the directorship of another Japanese designer, Nigo, moves easily between the world of French haute couture and the street. Nigo, to make this point, produces not only for Kenzo, but he has created spinoffs, such as Human Made, where the garments are designed with the street in mind. See, in this regard, Marx's *Ametora*.

6. There is also, since the war, a black American appropriation of the Ivy aesthetic. Bebop jazz artists such as John Coltrane, movie stars such Harry Belafonte and Sidney Poitier, and even Muhammad Ali all interpreted Ivy League preppiness in their own way, each adding his own particular edge. My favorite interpreter, however, is Miles Davis. In the 1950s, Miles could be seen in a sharp Brooks Brothers suit or looking louche in his button-down shirts. See, in addition to W. David Marx's work, *Black Ivy: A Revolt in Style*, edited by Jason Jules, graphics by Graham Marsh (Reel Art Press, 2021).

shirts, khakis, sweatshirts, hoodies, lettered sweaters, lettered varsity jackets, penny loafers; think Ralph Lauren's Polo shirts, sweater vests, chinos (like JFK and the era of Camelot). All of this often adorned with eye-catching patches (what was historically necessary now being paid homage to; out of historical fidelity comes cutting-edge fashion) and maybe a little on the baggy side (EG is especially good at this), when it is made in Japan. But today *boro* culture is also inspired by skateboarding, think southern California board shorts, loose garments, and of course, US street culture—think oversized garments such as T-shirts, sweatshirts, baggy jeans, and baseball hats (baseball hats and trucker hats made to look "worn"; that is, when they're precisely the kind of hat that is so reimagined as to ensure that it will never be encountered at truck stop on the I80 corridor).

There is also a decided nod to the great American outdoors; again think Ralph Lauren, but this time his rugged Colorado (Vail) and American Southwest (borrowed from the Indigenous people, the Diné/Navajo in particular) aesthetic as well as an homage to American workwear. When it comes to workwear, a brand such as Carhartt enjoys a certain preeminence; collaboration between workwear brands made hip (rebranded) as well as sports/leisure wear seems to be an ever-expanding undertaking. (Recently, Carhartt seems to be a brand with whom many hip Japanese designers now collaborate. But Carhartt is by no means the only brand to enjoy the attention of Japanese designers.) Of course, sneaker culture is huge, so Adidas, Nike, New Balance, recognizing the potential for increasing market share, have long since jumped eagerly on the bandwagon. But at the heart of all these brands such as Kapital and Visvim is US denim. And when it comes to jeans, San Francisco Levis' denim is the undisputed master of the *boro* imagination. Prominently located on the cover of W. David Marx's *Ametora* is a pair of high-fashion Levis.

The ethos of *boro* culture in its industrialist form is what we are confronting in Stuckey's haste to dispose of "cranes" to the "salivating Japanese." The relentless drive for profit must not be allowed to obscure the ways in which that object, imbued with the ideology of wartime death, reveals itself as a creative force. That is, it shows itself as the immanence of ongoing modes of cultural exchange and appropriation, opening onto a materialist repurposing. In short, it is an aesthetic creativity that is massively indebted to historical violence and, in the critical moment, a creativity that is indebted to the lack of a viable economic alternative.

Bastard 1

WHAT *BORO* CULTURE GIVES US is an insight into how all creativity, all innovation, is in one way or another someone's, some project's, bastard child. A bastard child who might be unloved, but, as Edward understands, is not necessarily unwanted. As with every bastard child, there is the memory of trauma: the powerful memory in which the child is abandoned. Strictly speaking, Edward is not a bastard, but he retains a sharp sense of that moment at which he is abandoned by his father—the father who abandons the son and his mother for another woman. We will address the role that the trauma of abandonment plays in Edward's psyche later, but not before we recognize the other ways in which the "bastard" discourse manifests itself.

The thing about a "bastard" such as Edward is that, like any vulture capitalist, he doesn't shrink from a fight. As he tells Vivian, he likes a "challenge."

James Morse iterates his history to Edward and Vivian over their second dinner:

> I'll get to the point. I think you're trying to take over my company. Given your track record, if you get it, it's easy to guess you'll liquidate it. I don't want that to happen. I built this company up myself. I've run it for forty years. We're in bad shape right now, but we're going to get through it . . .

Morse is not going to make Edward's most recent hostile take-over bid "easy." And, James Morse is, if not exactly a street fighter, then certainly a pugnacious late industrial capitalist; sort of a Jimmy Cagney in a moderately priced businessman's suit. Most important to James Morse, however, is his commitment to (his, metonymically speaking) late industrial capitalism. Given Edward's track record, it's not only that he will almost certainly liquidate Morse Industries but that Morse Industries is the last of a dying breed. Structured as it is, still committed to making things, Morse Industries is an anachronism, and Edward Lewis, very much a man of his time, is impatient with relics.

And so, as both James Morse and Edward know only too well, the older man is suffering from the economic delusion that Morse Industries can keep flying the flag of late industrial capitalism. Edward holds all the cards. He has stock in Morse Industries, and he has political capital in high places: the US Senate. It does not, for this reason, matter that Morse Industries is on the verge of securing another contract to build ten more ships for the US Navy. As soon as Edward catches wind of this, he has Stuckey contact a senator to make sure that the contract is not awarded to Morse Industries. Well, not yet, anyway. Edward wants the contract held up in Senate "appropriations." Were Morse Industries to secure the government contract before Edward's hostile take-over, the value of the company would increase, pushing up the value of the stock, thereby ensuring that Edward would have to pay much more for a company that is now ripe for his acquisition and at a price he likes, that is, a price at which he can reap maximum profits:

> Anyhow, we figure Morse Industries is worth about 400 million. We hope we can acquire it for between two and three hundred million. No matter what, I'm going to make a profit. The question is how large.

Ruthless vulture capitalist that he is, Edward is under no illusions as to what it is he does. As he tells Vivian after their first unsuccessful meeting with the Morses, "We're the same, Vivian, you and I. We both screw people for money." Except, of course, that their profit margins are vastly different. For Edward the "question is how large"—"between two and three hundred million": that is how much he stands to make, making of the $3,000 that he is paying her to escort him for the week, as the saying goes, "chicken feed," a matter of no financial consequence, certainly not for a PEF such as Edward. The difference is obscene, which seems to be the only goal that PEFs pursue, their very *raison d'etre*. Vivian, a quick (economic) study,[1] grasps Edward's logic, and, it must be said, seems to admire the rate of return his line of business can command. It's enough to make a working girl envious:

> **VIVIAN:** So you can make all that money just by buying it and then selling everything?
>
> **EDWARD:** Something like that.
>
> **VIVIAN:** What a racket! It sounds so easy.

1. Vivian's speed of thought is a feature that attaches to Julia Roberts in her 2000 movie, *Erin Brockovich,* for which she won an Oscar for Best Actress. Hollywood's reprising of certain features of an actor's key role is known as "mediatization," so that the actor carries those features into future roles, thereby maximizing what Richard Dyer refers to as "star power" (Dyer, *Heavenly Bodies: Film Stars and Society* [Routledge, 2003]). The actor's salient (marketable) features and the integration of those features into future roles come to constitute a singular whole, what might today be named as "branding." In short, Julia Roberts will, with rare exceptions, carry the aura of Vivian with her, ad infinitum. (As will, say, Robert De Niro carry the aura of Travis Bickle fom *Taxi Driver,* and Tom Cruise will retain elements of Peter Mitchell in *Top Gun* into future roles.)

It is, as Edward is at pains to point out, not quite as "easy" as it sounds, what with all the negotiations, the political skullduggery, and the backroom wheeling and dealing. Still, the contrast could not be sharper: $300 million (potentially) as opposed to $3,000. A difference on the order of a magnitude too mindboggling to contemplate.

It is an economic contrast made all the sharper if we recognize that Vivian actually puts her body to work—puts her body on the line, on a daily basis—while Edward has a vast corps of highly trained, well-paid minds (accountants, a research team, to say nothing of his secretary and other support staff) to perform both the specialized and the drudge labor for him. Philip Stuckey included, although as Edward's attorney, Stuckey is very well remunerated; so well remunerated, we would do well to remember, that he can afford that Lotus Esprit.

A New Economy of the Prostitute and Its Dangers

ALERT TO THE DISCREPANCIES IN WEALTH (and the vastly different modes of physical labor it takes to acquire that wealth), *Pretty Woman* imagines a new the economy of the prostitute by offering a critique of the traditional figures in the economy of prostitution—prostitute, john, pimp. (In the process, we can say, the movie reconfigures the function of the prostitute by making of her, in Žižek's terms, a moral actor.)

The roommates Vivian and her fellow-prostitute Kit do not have a pimp. It is more cost efficient, they recognize, to be their own economic advocates; although, of course, it makes their line of work more dangerous, because there is no one to protect them should the need arise; as it often does with johns who will, for example, not pay or who will do violence to the women. And the potential for violence is made all too clear at the beginning of *Pretty Woman* when Vivian spots the high heeled shoe of a dead prostitute in a dumpster outside the Las Palmas, a cheap motel complex close to where they live. Turns out that the murdered prostitute is a woman whom Kit knew, even though Kit dismisses her as a "crack whore," more or less. Vivian and Kit, the latter of whom introduced the smalltown girl from Georgia to the streets and showed her the ropes, are therefore bound to be each other's protection, a risk they are willing to take. They keep everything they earn. Taking risks is in keeping with Vivian's mode of being because, as she tells Edward in an early exchange, she's a "fly-by-the-seat-of-my-pants kinda girl."

In her encounter with Edward, however, their short circuiting the economy of the prostitute works to Vivian's (and later Kit's) advantage. An economic free agent, Vivian can negotiate her own terms, allowing her to move freely between the street and the (one-off opportunity to ply her trade in a) luxurious high-rise hotel where Edward is taking up temporary residence. Vivian's freedom of movement enables her to maximize her profit, to work wherever the going rate is best. And, because of the violence to which prostitutes are exposed, her contract with Edward is not only financially lucrative, but the upscale hotel—as opposed to the seedy motel of death—is almost completely safe, at least in physical terms.

But not, we should add, entirely. And the source of the violence belongs not to a random john cruising the less desirable parts of LA, but to Edward's expensively dressed but decidedly unlikable lawyer, Stuckey. Already angry at Vivian for prodding Edward, in his negotiations with Morse Industries, in the direction of preservation (of the Morses' company) rather than liquidation (the conventional PEF strategy), Stuckey the lawyer (a profession enamored of a "sharp, useless look," according to Vivian) first assaults Vivian verbally before trying to force her to have sex with him. It's what she does anyway, Stuckey reasons. In other words, Stuckey tries to rape her. Edward happens upon the scene, punches Stuckey, thus sparing Vivian from Stuckey's assault. The prostitute, as those who study the profession have long insisted, is not safe anywhere. They are fair game to everyone, regardless of socioeconomic status.

At the Regent Beverly Wilshire hotel, where the prostitute's dream and nightmare coexist cheek by jowl, lavish seduction (and seclusion) and brutal rape are but an encounter—a single individual—away.

My Fair Lady, Beverly Hills Style

AT LEAST AT THE BEGINNING OF HER STAY with Edward at the Regent, Vivian, dressed as she is in her working-girl attire, perpetually chewing gum, attracts all the wrong kind of attention. The other hotel guests subject her to accusatory looks, impolite sneers, and more than a few withering glances. She is saved from this fate soon after, in part because Edward, entrusting her with his credit cards, takes her to fancy boutiques so that she can, in a fashion distinct from but reminiscent of George Bernard Shaw's Eliza Doolittle of *Pygmalion* fame (remade by Lerner and Loewe into the musical *My Fair Lady*), be "cleaned up," made respectable. All of which makes her, of course, even more desirable to the likes of Philip Stuckey.

All a Pretty Prostitute Needs Is Her Own Dr. Henry Higgins

TO UNDERSTATE THE MATTER, all that the outspoken, opinion-ated Cockney (a working-class area in east London) woman Eliza Doolittle needed, of course, was a lesson in elocution. Vivian Ward, by contrast, needs a great deal more, not only how to speak the idiom of the Regent but how to speak that idiom without chewing gum. At no point, however, does Edward censor her. She is, at least in relation to him, free to speak her mind. A freedom she exercises to the fullest. (And she does so at least once, as we will see shortly, to the advantage of Morse Industries and late industrial capitalism.) Vivian must not only learn how to dress, but she must be instructed how to dress appropriately (that is, conform to bourgeois norms of respectability); not only how to dress, but how to dress tastefully, how to put aside her miniskirts and wear a demure and fetching brown-with-cream-polka dots sundress. Not only how to wear jewelry, but to choose the most flattering, discreet necklace.

In this regard, Vivian Ward has her own Mr. Henry Higgins, the professor of phonetics who instructs Eliza into perfect speech. The Henry Higgins function in *Pretty Woman* is performed by the Regent's suave, understated and paternal (at least in relation to "Ms. Vivian") concierge, Barnard "Barney" Thompson (Hector Elizondo). (Barney is much less enamored of "Ms. Kit de Luca.") "Barney," as "Ms. Vivian" is given to calling him, with unfailing and genuine exuberance (which contains more than a hint of gratitude and affection) provides a crash course in manners. "Barney" takes it upon himself to teach "Ms. Vivian" how to use expensive silverware, glassware, how to conduct herself in the rarefied environs of his hotel.

At heart, however, Vivian is still a working-class woman, sometimes finding herself ignorant of ruling-class etiquette. Sometimes she really doesn't know which fork to use. For which Barney really cannot be blamed. After all, he only had so much time, and game as she is as a student, Barney couldn't do much more than provide a quick primer in the art of manners.

And this is good luck for James Morse and his grandson, it turns out, because Vivian finds in James Morse, putatively, someone equally in need of instruction from a Ms. Manners or a Dr. Higgins.

The Upside of Not Knowing Which Fork to Use

AT EDWARD'S DINNER with James and David Morse, to which Edward has requested Vivian accompany him, Vivian struggles with the many items of cutlery that form part of her place setting. Struggling with one item, Vivian is saved by James Morse who declares himself, old school gallant that he is, equally befuddled by which fork to use first. As such, he dispenses with formality, ditches the fork, and takes the appetizer firmly in hand. Relieved, Vivian goes one better. She scrapes the appetizer clean, with a fork (the wrong one, no doubt), and follows James Morse's example.

The ice thus broken, socially, Edward and the Morses are able to find common economic ground. But Vivian's work is not yet done.

Morse Industries is spared the wrath of PEF, with some restructuring, of course, and James Morse leaves Edward and David to their discussion while he and Vivian engage in a pleasant tête-à-tête.

To save late industrial capital from the guillotine of postindustrialism, it helps if you do not know which piece of silverware to use.

If only it were that simple.

Who's Driving Edward Lewis?

EDWARD LEWIS, as we know, is out of his depth when it comes to industrial machinery. That much is inarguable. On taking Vivian up to his penthouse suite at their first meeting, he fumbles with the plastic card that will allow them entry. "I miss keys," Edward laments. As we know, he is even worse with high-end, expensive machinery. Of the vehicular variety. No surprise, because, as Edward acknowledges, "My first car was a limousine." The Lotus, Vivian tells an uncomprehending Edward, corners "like it's on rails."

Cornering like a Formula One driver is what girls from Georgia learn by regularly reading *Road and Track* magazine. Dumbfounded not only at her skill as a driver but by her knowledge of cars, Edward asks: "How do you know so much about cars?" "How do you know so little?" she shoots back, throwing Edward for more than a second.

Indeed, how does he know so little? Postindustrialist that he is—well, quite easily, actually. After all, one of the distinguishing features of the postmodern economy is that it moved from industrialization (mechanization) to technologization, from the assembly line to the mainframe computer to, in our moment, that all-purpose device, the cell phone (or, as a generation born with no use for the landline telephone would abbreviate—truncate—it, simply, the phone).

Having just been dumped by his latest girlfriend, who complains that she speaks to Edward's secretary Susan more than she does to him (it's a common Edward failing, as a former girlfriend attests) and finding himself in need of an escort for the week, Edward hires Vivian. Her rate, Edward finds out to his surprise, is $100 an hour. In response to Edward's astonishment, Vivian retorts: "I never joke about money." Edward, now back on more familiar turf, offers a quick and honest reply: "Neither do I."

Indeed, who, in the contemporary economy can afford to "joke about money?" Money is what gets you to the penthouse. Money is what can get you off the street—if you want, that is.

Bastard 2: The Hostility of the Takeover

EDWARD: It used to be easy. The market crash and a few scandals have made things tougher. And management has got smarter. I have to be more careful about my targets now.

—*Pretty Woman*

TO JAMES MORSE, Edward Lewis is nothing more than a "parasite." To label Edward as such, however, is to cast an effective moral aspersion, but it is also to understate both his ruthlessness and his appetite for consumption. Edward is a very large vulture, circling menacingly above distressed companies, occasionally toying with them by pretending to stage a takeover only to pull back at the very last moment. At other moments he is a brutal predator, taking exactly what he wants, picking the meat off the carcass of his victim, so to speak, and leaving naught but a bare bones in his wake.

When James Morse tells Edward that he knew his father, from whom Edward was estranged for the past "fourteen and a half years" of his father's life, and tells him that Edward's father was a "bastard," Edward demurs. He demurs because he claims the mantle of the bloodless PEF "bastard" for himself. Having already been rendered etymologically impure by James Morse, Edward goes one step further: "No," Edward says, "I've got the monopoly on that." Edward Lewis: the bastard's bastard. It's quite a thing to claim for oneself, a moniker most would prefer not to be appended to them. Whatever the poetry of "Greed is good," "bastard" has a sting that cannot be matched. What a thing it is to embrace it without apology.

In the PEF world, "bastards" always seem to come out on top. At least if you're named "Edward Lewis."

The enduring lesson of capital, however, is that it *extracts*, in one form or another. It never fails to get something, to take something from you, and never in a fair exchange for what you understand yourself to be giving it. In capitalism there is never an equal rate of return on the investment.

Edward knows this, and he uses his insight to damn Stuckey in their final encounter.

Angry after Edward manhandled him off Vivian while he was trying to rape her, Stuckey protests: "I gave you ten years." "Bullshit," Edward retorts, "you lived for the kill."

Et tu, Brute.

But to his own bloodlust, if not to his thirst for destructive destruction (to reconfigure Schumpeter), Edward is blind. His is a bloodlust that includes the blood of the father that is on his own hands.

Oedipal Drama,
Pretty Woman Style

EDWARD, however, is not only a capitalist "bastard" but, in his own quasi-Oedipal way, a de facto "bastard" too. It turns out that *Pretty Woman* is something of a Lewis family drama—family tragedy too, according to the terms of conventional tragedy as founded upon a tragic, irreparable, loss or injury that turns out to be life-altering: the murder of King Hamlet or the destruction of a black community in the work of Toni Morrison's *Song of Solomon* or *Paradise*. As Edward explains to Vivian, in the comfort of the luxurious bath they're sharing, his father abandoned his mother for another woman, taking the older Mr. Lewis's wealth with him. Edward's mother died afterward, although it is not clear how much being dumped for another woman had to do with it.

Edward being Edward, however, he got his revenge. The third company he took over, he tells Vivian, without any ostensible glee, was his father's, in relation to which he behaved in a thoroughly Edwardian fashion. We presume he treated it as he did the first two companies he liquidated, and as he is now promising to do to Morse Industries: He broke it up and sold it—at a profit, of course. In *Pretty Woman*, at least, maybe it is not vulture capitalism we're talking about. Maybe it is better understood as revenge capitalism. The only way to kill the father is to take from him the very thing that he spent his life building. In so doing, the son—rather than behaving in the normative Oedipal terms by killing the father so as to possess the love object (the mother)— instead avenges the mother, post facto: revenging the mother in death by putting the father to death, financially. Psychologically, too, by being the instrument of economic wrath. Hell hath no fury like a son abandoned. Pity the industrial capitalist father.

The love that the son lost when his father abandoned him and his mother cannot be retrieved, so that the lost love becomes the weaponized object of nostalgia. Nostalgia, that is, on the order of the Rolling Stones: "You can't always get what you need / But if you try sometimes, you just might get what you need." And what Edward needs, at least in this particular iteration of the Oedipal drama, is to render the unloving father without his love object. The elder Mr. Lewis is free to hang on to his ill-gotten gains (his second wife), but the source of his wealth, the denial of which became the source of Edward's (relative, we presume) impover-ishment (no more limos), is violently wrenched away from him.

Edward could not regain his father's love, as is evidenced by his long estrangement (fourteen and a half years; no final goodbyes—"I wasn't there when he died"), but he got what he needed: revenge. The son learned the value of capital extraction and, to phrase the matter in Schumpeter's terms, the son learned the art of "creative destruction," which becomes the denoue-ment, the brutal twist in the tale, or the final twist in a brutal generational revenge saga.

Making and Unmaking in the
Oedipal Family Drama

IN THE ORDINARY OEDIPAL PSYCHODRAMA OF FAMILY LIFE, the son kills the father. However, within the logic of late industrial capitalism, with its anachronistic imperative to "make something," to "build something here," this is how the son *makes* something of himself. By killing the father's late industrialist company (the "old man's dream," as the *Fils renard* of *Wall Street* might have been tempted to phrase it), the son lays waste to the father. The aggressive teleology of capitalism, the determination to always be innovative, a capitalism that is relentless in its pursuit of the new, the drive that sustains capitalism, functions analogically here. The son makes of the father's economic pursuit, what should constitute the immanence of the father's legacy, not only an anachronism but renders the father himself, and how he is in the world as a capitalist, obsolete.

That is how your kill your father. Dead.

The father is thus subjected to two (consecutive) deaths. The first is the putting to death of his mode of production and, because of the brutal decisiveness of that death, making immanent to the father his (economic) obsolescence. The second, physical (actual laying to rest), death is rendered inconsequential. If, as it is said, cowards die many deaths before their death, then we can say that late industrial capitalists are not so fortunate. They are permitted only one death, and it is a death that condemns them to an economic afterlife that serves no purpose other than to remind them of their (economic) irrelevance. Their mode of production has been made irrelevant by the new modes of capital acquisition.

In Biblical terms, the late industrial capitalist reaps both more and less than he sowed. He is rewarded for his economic production (the price of the buyout that, as we know from Edward's negotiations with Morse Industries, is not insubstantial; in other words, the industrial capitalist profits), but that always amounts to less than the inestimable value of having "built something." And we know from both James and David Morse, the elder of whom must be understood here as standing analogically in relation to the late Mr. Lewis, that there is no price that can be put on the value of having "built something."

It is this desperation, this immersion in, identification with, and attachment to a mode of capitalist production that has become an irritant (and, in some ways an impediment to) postindustrial capital, that we hear in James Morse's plaintive cry: "We make things." "We build Navy destroyers." (It must be said, with these the US Navy potentially wreaks destruction on other peoples in the world. Are we then, facetiously, to be glad that vulture capitalism puts paid, at least in this instance, to one mode of death? That one part of the military-industrial complex is suspended, if only for that moment of its transition from late industrial capitalism to postindustrial capitalism?) Vulture capitalism unmakes what it is industrial capitalism used to pride itself on making.

The son has unmade the father. Edward plays, to a tee, the deadly (economic) game of exceeding the father. As know all too well, the logic of legacy is widespread among the ruling classes.

This is a logic governed by the imperative of infinite surpassing/excess. The offspring will always succeed in exceeding the parents; the offspring's generation, which will acquire the skills requisite to its era, will increase the family fortune. By these standards of success, if by no other, Edward emerges victorious. He triumphs not only in terms of generating new modes of wealth, but he succeeds in showing the economic obsolescence of his father's generation.

This is how the son makes something of himself. This is how the (unmaking of the) father proves to be the making of the son.

To Make Something

DEAD AS THE FATHER HAS BEEN MADE BY THE SON—twice over, no less—the son cannot banish the father. The son remains, therefore, haunted by what he is not making. Or, that he is *Not. Making. Something.*

That Morse Industries is saved for late industrial capitalism, that it will continue to make something is not, as one might be tempted to argue (contrary to Stuckey's firm belief), due to Vivian's arrival in Edward's life. The vulture capitalist losing his way from Philip Stuckey's mansion to the Regent Beverley Wilshire and landing up, after midnight, in the bad part of town, is not the road to Damascus, not of the late industrial capitalist variety, anyway.

Whatever role Vivian plays is a philosophical one. It is Vivian's refusal to disarticulate the moral from the ethical that enables her to bring to life what has long been latent in Edward, longer than even fourteen and a half years. Latent in Edward are the residues of a dead father who continues to haunt the bastard son. Vivian functions as the spur of ethical discomfiture and difficulty that has long been brewing in Edward.

However, ethical catalyst—of sorts, the spark that lights the ethical fire, if you prefer—though she be, Vivian can have no place in the patronymic drama, and certainly not in its resolution.

The patronymic, the bastard son determined—unsuccessfully, of course—to shuck off the father's imprint on him. In order to do so, the son must contain the confrontation with the father. Above all, it must be private, though its effects will show themselves to be intensely public. And, the patronymic drama, against the backdrop that is the absent presence of the dead father, must be staged through the surrogate, one who is, of course, never acknowledged as a surrogate, as substitute for the absent-present dead father.

Edward and James Morse face off in private after Edward has cleared the boardroom of everyone. Edward asks everyone to leave him and James Morse alone. Stuckey, understanding himself indispensable to Edward, remains seated and is visibly upset (the fraternal rejection of Stuckey? Or, the loss of the love object for Stuckey? Both may very well be true) and can hardly bring himself to leave. Edward is happy to allow David Morse to remain, but James Morse, recognizing the significance of Edward's need for complete privacy, has his grandson leave. David makes a graceful exit, unlike the churlish, spurned Stuckey.

James Morse is expecting a struggle, and he is ready for combat.

But Edward surprises him. Morse Industries will not be spared this hostile (but not too hostile) takeover, but it will be allowed to continue to build ships. To make the things it has been making for forty years.

As James Morse, full of goodwill having been spared the guillotine that is vulture capitalism, says to everyone upon their return to the boardroom: "We're going to build ships, great big ships." Stuckey, as one might imagine, is not best pleased. Edward has betrayed not only Stuckey but the very im-moral principle upon which their relationship is founded: Not do unto others, but undo (unto) them; what they have built, have made. "Greed," and destructive destruction, "is good." It is the supreme principle.

The key articulation, the signal exchange, between Edward and James Morse, however, is not Edward's betrayal of the principle of destructive destruction. It is rather that moment when, grasping that Morse Industries has been granted, against all his and his grandson's expectations, a new, economically viable lease of life, James Morse—standing face-to-face with Edward—says, almost quietly: "I'm proud of you, son."

For the briefest of moments, the patrilineal line has been restored.

The bastard son, in saving the surrogate father who is not a surrogate father but is a surrogate father, reclaims for himself a father of/from the industrialist era.

Is this all what the bastard son wanted all along?

Father's Son, Mother's Son: The Enduring Phantasmatic Father

IN THE PROCESS OF PUTTING THE FATHER TO DEATH, the bastardization of the bastard son is confirmed, out of which emerges the question of economic paternity. If the industrial economy is being destroyed by the bastard son, does this not make of all capital an illegitimate offspring (gain)? What is capital without paternity? Nasty, brutish, and everlasting?

Are we now free to declare, long after it is we should have done so, that all capital accumulation is illegitimate? Against parental, that is to say, God's law?

What does the bastard son stand to inherit but his father's ill-gotten gains? Must the mother and the father die so that the son can make of his bastardy a public declaration? Is it only when the father has been killed, laid to industrialist rest (that is, made subject to his first death), that the bastard son can pro-/claim, "I am not—I am no longer—my father's son?"

This in the face of the immanent truth that is: The bastard son remains always, despite his every striving, his father's son.

A futile gesture, in truth, because the son, avenging angel though he be, cannot resurrect the mother. The mother cannot be brought back to life. What is the bastard son to do, then, but seek his own validation through attaching himself to the Mary Magdalene figure that the fates present to him? Lost though he be, unable to find his way to his putative destination, the Regent Beverley Wilshire, he returns to it in the company of the wayward, lost daughter, the young woman from the New South who keeps herself alive through ill-begotten gains. Is it only the maligned Mary Magdalene who can restore the ethical to the bastard son? The fiction, the frisson, of the mother returned to nurture and to love, to nurture into self-love.

The self that must be made to turn to the work of making. The self that must, as if from the ground up, make itself into an ethical self that is felicitous to its own ethics. Self-making, on the order of Michel Foucault. Intellectually rigorous (Athens), severely disciplined (Spartan), scrupulously attaching itself to that desire which is unfailingly true. True to the imperative of philosophy's first principle: know thyself.

The mother is invoked. Mourned, even. Grieved over, after which the son appears able to continue his life. But it is the father, as phantasm, as the amalgam of an absent-presence, a distinct kind of surrogacy, and the specter of Glissantian reversion-diversion, who haunts the bastard son. It is against the phantasmatic father that the bastard son sets himself, whom the bastard son seeks to undo only to find himself acceding to the very modality of capitalism that he is intent upon liquidating.

It is the phantasmatic father who makes possible the surrogate father's ebullient declaration: "We're going to build ships, great big ships." By throwing an economic lifeline to Morse Industries, the bastard son resurrects not only almost-dead late industrial capitalism, but he brings the phantasmatic father back to life.

Who is it, exactly, saying, "I'm proud of you, son?" To which father do those words belong? Is it the phantasmatic father speaking through—as, with the words of—the surrogate father?

Is it only by, finally, agreeing to make something that the bastard son can speak to the father? Is this way as direct as possible to access the speaking of the phantasmatic father? Is life to be found in the entanglement that is the phantasmatic father?

At the very least, we can say that it is in the figure of James Morse that the phantasmatic father is re-turned to us. "Mr." Lewis is the father who is never afforded a proper name; that is, he is not made distinct from the son. "Mr." Lewis is the father who cannot be named, who is made unnameable by the son, is reduced to and therefore rises up asf a voluble, disruptive anonymity by the son. The son who contains within him the only living fragment of the phantasmatic father.

Within this figure of James Morse, the fragments, bastard son and disruptively anonymous father, find their entanglement. James Morse is that entanglement that brings into exchange the tangible fragment—the ships that Morse Industries will now be able to continue building—and the without-immanence whole that is postindustrial capitalism.

The phantasmatic father that is late industrial capitalism, we recognize, has been given a reprieve. Only a reprieve. The phantasmatic father will be doomed to extinction. Again. Only to assume a new-old guise. Perhaps even to, in the most phantasmatic way, place in the stead of the dead father an aging surrogate. The surrogate father who pronounces himself "proud" of the bastard son, the surrogate who can be spared the violence enacted against the absent-present (first) father. The phantasmatic father makes himself a present absence, lending his in-visibility the quality of the specter. The phantasmatic father allows himself to be seen, this time through the refraction that is surrogacy, thereby raising the possibility of the nostalgic.

The phantasmatic father will, as such, make himself always available as political instrument. The phantasmatic father will always have to live, in death, with the prospect of being asked to resurrect himself (itself?) back into (postindustrialist) life, to leap out of and over death, back into life. The phantasmatic father can, then, never be laid to rest. The phantasmatic father is too valuable an ideological asset to be declared dead and buried forever.

The phantasmatic father is, ultimately, the most enduring artifact that the bastard son has produced. The bastard son, in the act of leaping backward as only the patronymic allows, has made himself his father's father.

No one, beginning with James Morse, can never again accuse Edward Lewis of not making something.

The bastard son has shown himself capable of extracting a benign late industrial Frankenstein out of the postindustrial wreckage that he, Mr. Edward Lewis, and the phantasmatic "Mr. Lewis," in their brutal entanglement, hath wrought. Out of death, life. After a manner.

The Žižekian Ethics of
Mick Jagger

STILL, IT IS MICK JAGGER'S QUESTION THAT HAUNTS: Is this what Edward wants? We can safely say that, at least in economic and (petty) Oedipal terms, Edward has gotten what he needs. *Pretty Woman*, however, has the distinction of making of Mick's question an ethical one, ethical in the Žižekian register. Not only, an ethical question, however, but an ethics that cannot be disarticulated from Žižekian morality. In strict, by which I mean perverse, Žižekian terms, Edward has behaved morally toward his father. In fact, Edward has been more moral—again, perversely so—than his father. He has done more unto his father than his father did unto him. Live by industrial capitalism, die by postindustrial capital.

The ethical kernel of the Mick Jagger–Slavoj Žižek question, however, is a different one. A fundamental one, even. Is Edward behaving in a felicitous way with his desires? Succinctly phrased, what does Edward *want*? This is the ethical difficulty that *Pretty Woman* poses and, it must be said, the movie answers. At least in one register.

By the end of *Pretty Woman* we can say this about Vivian. The small-town girl from Georgia can distinguish between what she needs, even if only as a negation, and what she wants. What she needs is not to be Edward's kept woman. When, on their final day together, Edward suggests that he will furnish Vivian with an apartment, a driver, and credit cards so that she can shop to her heart's content, she refuses. When Edward insists to Vivian that "I have never treated you as a prostitute," she responds, almost in a whisper, out of his earshot, "You just did."

To be a kept woman, a former prostitute on (a handsome) retainer, as it were, is what Vivian does not need. What she wants, as she tells Edward on the balcony of the penthouse suite, is the "fairytale." The knight—or, as Vivian would prefer, the "prince"—on a white horse who rescues the damsel in distress and whisks her away to . . . well, in this case, a destination to be determined. The fairytale1 is not, needless to say, what Edward is proposing, and Vivian walks away from what would seem a very sweet deal.

"It Must Be Very Difficult to Let Go of Something So Beautiful"

"IT MUST BE VERY DIFFICULT to let go of something so beautiful." This line belongs, as it properly should, to the concierge-sage Barney Thompson. It is a remark, resonant with romantic meaning (giving up Vivian's love), that Barney offers to Edward when Edward asks him to return to the store the jewelry (a necklace and a pair of earrings) that Edward had borrowed for Vivian to wear to their night at the opera in San Francisco. Barney, consummate professional that he is, of course agrees, after which he offers his insight, thereby setting in motion Edward's ride (in a limousine, of course) back to the wrong side of town, where Vivian's apartment is.

Having decided that he cannot, after all, "let go of something so beautiful," Edward now has to overcome his acrophobia. Vivian doesn't, of course, live in a penthouse, but Edward does have to brave, in his expensively tailored suit, two flights of rickety, poorly maintained, iron stairs. Cheap, bodega-bought red roses in hand, Edward duly performs his chivalrous duty. "Cinda-fucking-rella," as Kit describes the phenomenon, is rescued. By rescuing her, Edward gives Vivian what she wants.

Whereupon the tables are turned, and Edward is given something.

89

We know Edward's business ethics. His desire is for money and more money. Power, political influence at the highest levels of the US government, these are for him a means to his ethical end. Power and political influence allow him to be continuously felicitous to his ethics. But, the question persists, is this what he wants? *Pretty Woman* suggests that the ethical is, at best, a composite whole, better apprehended in its fragmentation, recognized as comprising more than one strand.

The other ethical strand, the one that escapes Edward's grasp, is the one that Vivian makes immanent to him, one that *only* Vivian can make immanent. Edward's "ex-wife," who now "lives in his ex-house with his ex-dog on Long Island," could not make this immanent. Neither could the string of rich socialite girl-friends, including his most recent ex. What needs to be made immanent to Edward is the economy of un-equal exchange. "Un-equal" because it operates in a register—"love" is the only name we can give it—in which there is no room for the discourse of profit and loss, because it is nothing if not an imprecise, specu-lative, life-affirming metric. (This is Hollywood, after all.) To commit to the un-equal is to give to the other with the expecta-tion of reciprocation that is never guaranteed. Love is that risk where every gesture, every act of giving to the other, every act of self-sacrifice, every exchange, intimate or not, is fraught with the possibility of inequality—there is no guarantee that the other will respond in kind or, of course, equal measure. Love is the ultimate form of speculation. Loving the other always involves the risk of squandering the self—the only capital that has any currency in love—in the cause of the other.

Love locks the self and the other into the economy of un-equal exchange. Love habituates self and other into a bond of un-equal exchange. Love is the contracting of the self into an un-equal bond with the other. Love, as Shakespeare might say, has no measure and so does not bear refutation. Or, denial, as Edward finds out. Faced with the prospect of losing Vivian, Edward directs the limousine driver—Daryl—to Vivian's neighborhood. Thereby finding what he was on the cusp of losing.

Vivian, who is totally committed to the un-equal, offers Edward the best possible deal, gives him the only guarantee she can. Vivian's is the Cinderella economy that strives to install the equal, as far as is possible, at the core of the relationship to the other.

Having rescued Cinderella, Edward asks, quite naively (as if he is not really expecting an answer), "Then what does she [Cinderella] do?" Vivian's answer catches Edward off guard, a matter for some concern for Edward's physical well-being because he is precariously balanced on the rickety landing: "She rescues him right back."

From the moment that *Pretty Woman* transforms Edward from a ruthless vulture capitalist into a bastard, it is unarguable that, as Vivian surely intuits, while Edward can get everything that he needs, he needs a lot of help in trying to understand what he wants.

(What a disappointment Edward must be to Mick and Keith: he can always get what he needs, he just doesn't know what he wants.)

Hence, the rescue operation. In saving Cinderella, the prince himself is saved. Except that this Cinderella's prince doesn't know what he wants, at least not in any way that would suggest he is beginning to know it.

Let us name the economy of un-equal exchange the complementary ethical strand: the other revealing to the self what it is the self wants because the self itself does not know what it wants. Such ethics, as it were, is not only as felicitous to the self's desires but as the possibility of the self's being instructed into what it should be felicitous to. In a word, Edward does not know what he wants so he must be taught ethics, an admonition at once as preposterous and searingly appropriate as it sounds—teaching ethics through the un-equal that is love.

That such ethical work should fall to the prostitute is, in the architecture of *Pretty Woman,* not at all surprising. Vivian, unlike Edward, already operates in two registers, the moral and ethical, and for Vivian the ethical is not singular but operates as a composite structure. Vivian, unlike Edward, both has her feet on the ground (she walks the streets) even as her ethics locates her in a higher—perhaps even a lofty—place. Vivian does not suffer from acrophobia. Edward must, literally and ethically (figuratively) be instructed into how to ascend to those heights at which the various composite strands and their (incipient) entanglement can be glimpsed. Strands that are dangling, entangled, yet discrete; discrete but in need of being reconstituted into a provisional object—love. To see what is on the ground, Edward must be made to go up.

And not in a fancy elevator—not in the exclusive kind of hotels where elevator operators are still the norm—but under his own steam. Edward must make the ascent, literally, step by terrified step. In any case, the view from the penthouse may be too much for him. That way he'd have to look down into the abyss, and Vivian clearly understands that Edward, as he is happy to acknowledge, has his limits. "That is all I can offer," Edward says to Vivian when she refuses his offer to be kept by him. Looking down from Vivian's landing, his eyes betraying a palpable fear (love has not yet been able to cure acrophobia), between the first and the second floor of the Las Palmas hotel is, at that point, his maximum point of elevation.

To Steal, to Make of Steel

LOVE, to simultaneously invoke and invert Bob Dylan, is the "one direction home."[1] Instead of declaring that there is "no direction home," *Pretty Woman* instead presents the possibility that only love can show you the way, that the path that runs through the phantasmatic, through surrogacy. That is how you get to your purloined destination.

The only way to get to where you're supposed to be is to steal your way there, to steal from the phantasmatic father so as to give life to the surrogate father: love as stealth. As Edward finds out, Vivian can't be bought—well, not after a point, anyway.

But there is a way to steal his way into her heart.

By agreeing to make a "great big ship" that is made of steel.

By agreeing to build again, Edward makes it possible for his morality and the ethical to be brought, for what he hopes is a

---

1. *No Direction Home*—Bob Dylan (youtube.com) (February 7, 2024). This Martin Scorsese documentary of Dylan opens with a British fan asking Dylan for an autograph. Dylan, being Dylan, refuses, saying, "You don't need my autograph. If you did, I'd give it to you." Dylan recognizing that there is a significant existential difference between what the fan wants and what that fan needs. That which is needed must be given. That which is wanted is not to be granted. At least not in the ecosphere that is Bob Dylan's relationship to his fans.

sustained moment, into a perfect symmetry, one not so much lodged within the other as continuous with the other. The unity of fragments. Unity in the fragmentary. Sometimes you not only get what you need, but you also get what you didn't know you needed, that which you could never have imagined yourself to have wanted.

Just once, and that may be the best we hope for, we can claim that it is possible to prove Mick Jagger wrong.

Acknowledgments

My ability to shape this essay owes everything to Dr. Leah Pennywark. She helped me think the essay and then find out how it was that the essay needed to be written. And then, as I approached the end of the process, she pointed out, correctly, what it was the essay needed. Once more, Dr. Pennywark, my thanks.

As has become habitual for me now, I would like, one more time, to thank the finest minds in the Commonwealth of Pennsylvania: "Monsignor" Robert Caserio and Jeff Nealon. Not sure how much longer I can ask you to "put it on my tab." But ask I will. Thanks.

My friend and colleague Levon Barseghyan is an economist possessed of an acute cultural and political sensibility. Thanks for pointing me in the direction in which I needed to go.

Finally, this essay is dedicated to my uncles, maternal, Godfrey, and paternal, James and W. Arthur. For what it is and how it is they gave. Each distinct. Uncle James, who endured longest . . .

—Ithaca, 2023

(Continued from page iii)

Forerunners: Ideas First

P. David Marshall
The Celebrity Persona Pandemic

Davide Panagia
Ten Theses for an Aesthetics of Politics

David Golumbia
The Politics of Bitcoin: Software as Right-Wing Extremism

Sohail Daulatzai
Fifty Years of *The Battle of Algiers*: Past as Prologue

Gary Hall
The Uberfication of the University

Mark Jarzombek
Digital Stockholm Syndrome in the Post-ontological Age

N. Adriana Knouf
How Noise Matters to Finance

Andrew Culp
Dark Deleuze

Akira Mizuta Lippit
Cinema without Reflection: Jacques Derrida's Echopoiesis and Narcissism Adrift

Sharon Sliwinski
Mandela's Dark Years: A Political Theory of Dreaming

Grant Farred
Martin Heidegger Saved My Life

Ian Bogost
The Geek's Chihuahua: Living with Apple

Shannon Mattern
Deep Mapping the Media City

Steven Shaviro
No Speed Limit: Three Essays on Accelerationism

Jussi Parikka
The Anthrobscene

Reinhold Martin
Mediators: Aesthetics, Politics, and the City

John Hartigan Jr.
Aesop's Anthropology: A Multispecies Approach

Grant Farred is professor of Africana studies and English at Cornell University and the author of *Only a Black Athlete Can Save Us Now (Minnesota, 2022); An Essay for Ezra: Racial Terror in America* (Minnesota, 2021); *Martin Heidegger Saved My Life* (Minnesota, 2015), *In Motion, at Rest: The Event of the Athletic Body* (Minnesota, 2014), *What's My Name? Black Vernacular Intellectuals* (Minnesota, 2003), and *Midfielder's Moment: Coloured Literature and Culture in Contemporary South Africa.*